HOT RODS

HOT RODS

DAN BURGER, ROBERT GENAT, AND DAIN GINGERELLI

Lowe & B. Hould
Publishers

This edition published in 2004 by Lowe & B. Hould, in coordination with MBI Publishing Company.

First published by MBI Publishing Company.

Little Deuce Coupe © Robert Genat, 2002, 2004
Retro Rods © Dan Burger and Robert Genat, 2001, 2004
Ford Hot Rods ©Dain Gingerelli, 1998, 2004

ISBN 0-681-16613-4

Front cover: One of the most famous 1932 Ford coupes of all time is the one that John Milner drove in the movie, *American Graffiti*. For that movie, director George Lucas wanted a basic hot rod that would have been driven on the California streets in 1962. The car was originally found at a swap meet and was modified to suit Lucas' image. It survives today in its original form, including the license plate, THX138, an allusion to one of his early films.

On the frontispiece: When the Beach Boys released their *Little Deuce Coupe* album in 1962, Capitol Records executives picked Chili Catallo's 1932 Ford Coupe for the cover. Originally built for the street and strip in the late 1950s, the coupe was quickly converted into a show car with the help of legendary customizers George Barris and the Alexander Brothers. The son of the late owner currently owns this famous coupe.

On the title page: This '32 Ford coupe, stripped of fenders and finished in black primer, looks as if it's ready for a jalopy race or a fast run across one of California's dry lakes. Builders follow certain themes when constructing a hot rod. This '32 coupe looks like those built in the late 1950s or early 1960s.

On the back cover: Fenderless cars dominate the retro-rodders, but bobbed rear renders were not uncommon on the original roads. This rod was originally built in the late 1950s. After being driven for several years it was put away and forgotten until it was recently discovered. It still wears its original lime green paint.

Printed in China

CONTENTS

LITTLE DEUCE COUPE

RETRO RODS

FORD HOT RODS

LITTLE DEUCE
Coupe

ROBERT GENAT

Acknowledgments

Hot rodders, and especially deuce coupe owners, are the greatest group of guys in the world. The following '32 Ford coupe owners bent over backward to help me while I was photographing their cars, and they all have subsequently become friends. My thanks to Arden Honrud, Bill Lewis, Rick Cronin, Curt Catallo, George Stupar, John Bade, Mike Martin, Rick Figari, Alex "Axle" Idzardi, Aaron Kahan, Brent Bell, Bill Webb, Richard Lux, Jeff Vodden, Shaun Price, Gary Moline, Mike "Sparky" Sparks, Bob Berry, Sam Davis, Don Garlits, Bruce Meyer, John Guilmet, Garry Biddinger and Howard Gribble (whom I first saw on the San Diego freeway and chased for 40 miles before I could get him to pull over). Thanks to three gearheads who helped me with this book, Gary Jankowski, Gordie Craig, and Dan Burger. Thanks to my San Francisco "transportation captain," Creighton Laskey. A big thanks to Tony Thacker and the staff at the So-Cal Speed Shop and Darin Bond at Gibbon. And thanks to my friend David Newhardt for his excellent deuce photos.

One of my most memorable moments while producing this book was the time I met up with Rick Figari, owner of the yellow '32 five-window coupe used in the movie *American Graffiti*. We had arranged to meet in a parking lot near the Presidio in San Francisco. I was looking for an enclosed car trailer. As if on cue, I saw the yellow '32 coupe emerge from the fog and round the corner in my direction. Figari was tooling around in the most famous '32 coupe to ever grace the silver screen. Like a thousand other guys, I've had a love affair with this car since 1973. When I saw it in person, I had the thrill you get when you meet a sports or entertainment personality you've always admired. As with most personalities, the coupe looked better in person—and unlike a movie starlet, this one gets better with age.

Introduction

It was a bold move, but Henry Ford had a habit of making bold moves. As the Depression was tightening its hold on the nation's financial neck, Ford decided to introduce a new car. It was a new, inexpensive car with a V-8 engine. The new car and engine would cost the company a lot of money, but this project would keep most of Ford's workforce in place. Henry Ford didn't seem to care about spending the money, because he had it in the bank. He was more concerned about keeping the economy going and trying to regain the sales lead from Chevrolet. Ford felt that losing money in the stock market was a greater setback than losing money in the course of running a business. By manufacturing a new car, his workers would at least get paid a salary and would keep the economy going.

Throughout the 1920s, Ford had a successful run with the Model T and subsequent Model A. Henry Ford grudgingly added colors to the Model A, but kept the four-cylinder engine. In 1932 he would introduce a V-8 to one-up Chevrolet's six. At that time, V-8 engines were only installed in more expensive luxury cars. The cost to produce a V-8 was high. Ford didn't copy a design already in production, but designed an entirely new engine with a block that was cast as a single element. This design reduced the manufacturing cost, which made it practical for production. The fact that all the raw materials needed to build a car were inexpensive also contributed to the low cost. The cost of steel was at a 20-year low, copper was at a 30-year low, and aluminum had never been cheaper.

When Ford introduced its new car on March 31, 1932, it offered 14 models, including a station wagon, in both Standard and Deluxe trim. The car was a completely new design, rather than a Model A with a facelift. The '32 model was longer and lower than the Model A and had a more streamlined body. The windshield was slanted back at a rakish 10-degree angle and was no longer covered by a visor, a stylish grille shell surrounded the radiator, and the fuel tank was moved from the cowl to the rear of the car. The frame rails were exposed on the sides of the car above the running boards. With the optional V-8, the '32 Ford was fast. Road tests at the time clocked the new V-8 at 16.8 seconds from 0 to 60 miles per hour, with a top speed of 76 miles per hour.

Considering that the nation's economy was suffering through the worst part of the Depression in 1932, the new Fords sold well at slightly over 300,000 units. Sales, however, fell far short of the 1.5 million cars that Ford had predicted. Prices ranged from $410 for the four-cylinder Standard roadster to $650 for the V-8 powered station wagon.

The '32 Ford's classic lines had an enduring quality. The styling was refined, and the stock version of the car

Howard Gribble's chopped three-window high-boy has an aggressive stance due to big 'n' little tires mounted on Halibrand wheels.

was as fast as any other vehicle on the road. It had that undeniable "something special" that helped make it the favorite of hot rodders. Any Ford produced in 1932 soon came to be known as a "deuce," referring to the "2" in '32.

In the 1940s, the 1932 Ford was an inexpensive used car. For young me returning from the war, turning it into a hot rod was easy. The switch to a later, more powerful flathead was simple. Aftermarket manufacturers were soon making multicarb intakes, high-compression heads, and full-race camshafts for the flathead. In addition, Ford's 1940s-era production cars had upgraded chassis components, such as transmissions, rear ends, and hydraulic brakes, which were easily swapped to the '32. Dry lakes racers loved the deuce, because it could be easily fieldstripped of fenders and running boards for competition. Drag racers loved the car for the same reasons. On the street, the '32 looked good with or without the original fenders. For more variety, the bodies could be easily channeled down over the frame rails, and the tops could be chopped.

When the overhead V-8s became popular in the 1950s, hot rodders found that one would easily fit into the '32's ample engine compartment. The flathead soon made way for Chrysler Hemis, small-block Chevys, and Olds Rocket engines. Behind those engines were a variety of manual and automatic transmissions. Plates were added to the inside of the frame rails (boxing) to increase strength to hold the heavier engines. New cross-members were added to support the varied transmissions. As everything automotive improved, so did the deuce.

In the 1970s, the supply of solid deuce bodies and frames was dwindling. The laws of supply and demand took over, and soon several companies were building reproduction frames and bodies. The first bodies (roadsters) were crude and often ill proportioned. As the demand rose, several new manufacturers jumped in to build well-engineered chassis and dimensionally accurate bodies that included both styles of coupe. The world's favorite hot rod was again available to the masses.

Today the demand for a deuce-based hot rod is as high as ever. The mystique and charm of the '32 Ford continues today, as the children and grandchildren of original hot rodders experience the same love affair with the deuce. The '32 Ford, in any body style, will always be the quintessential American hot rod.

Chapter 1

The Original Deuce Coupes

Within weeks of its release, early hot rodders saw the potential of the new deuce. Its fresh styling and engine selection quickly made it a favorite. The new '32 featured a well-developed four-cylinder engine that could be easily modified, and a modern V-8 engine. Racers stripped off fenders and headlights in a crude attempt at streamlining to improve their running times at the dry lakes. For a long time, only roadsters were allowed to race on the dry lakes. Following World War II, coupes were allowed to race on the lakes, and '32 three- and five-windows were some of the first to do so. Tops were chopped to reduce drag and the fenders removed, developing the new highboy coupe look would set the standard for hot rod coupes for decades to come.

A small V-8 emblem graced the center of the headlight bar on all V-8-equipped 1932 Fords. All Deluxe models, such as this three-window, were equipped with cowl lights and a chromed windshield frame. The vertical grille bars on all '32s were painted French Gray.

When the new '32 Fords were introduced, there were two coupe models, the five-window Standard (B-45) and the three-window Deluxe (B-520). Each could be ordered with either a four-cylinder engine or the new V-8. The window arrangement of the five-window, called a "four-window" in 1932 sales literature, gave it the look of the Model A coupe, while the three-window had a look all of its own. Art deco was a strong design theme in the early 1930s, and the entire 1932 line, including the two coupes, embodied the art deco style. The bodies were made of steel with inner hardwood reinforcements. A fabric insert was fitted to the center of the roof, because the techniques required to stamp such a deep draw, or impression, into a large roof panel had not yet been developed. Both coupes came with a rear luggage compartment standard. For an additional $25, a two-passenger rumble seat was available in both versions. The rear window on both coupes could be lowered. In addition to excellent ventilation, this feature allowed convenient conversation with rumble seat passengers.

All 1932 Ford five-window coupes were built as Standard models. The Standard came with a black body and could be ordered in several optional colors, such as this Medium Maroon, but the fenders were always painted black. Colored wheels were a $5 extra cost option.

Both coupes rode on the same 106-inch wheelbase frame, which was 2.5 inches longer than the Model A. For 1932, the rear spring mount was positioned 6 inches behind the rear axle. This spaced the springs 112 inches apart. Ford's theory was that the car would ride better with the springs further apart. The wheels on the

'32 Fords were a drop center design with 32 welded spokes. Standard tires were 5.25X18 black sidewalls, with optional white sidewall tires. The front axle was a forged I-beam design supported by a transverse spring with 12 leaves. The rear spring on both coupes had 9 leaves. Mechanically actuated drum brakes were fitted

Both the three- and five-window coupes had a rumble seat for an option. It used the same deck lid as those coupes equipped with a luggage compartment, except it was hinged to open rearward. To facilitate entry to the rumble seat, round rubber step pads were added to the right rear bumper and to the top of the right rear fender. The rear window on all coupes rolled down for ventilation and to allow the front seat passengers to talk to those in the rumble seat.

on all four wheels, and the spare tire was mounted on the rear of the car.

Both the Standard and Deluxe coupes could be ordered as a Model B with the 50-horsepower four-cylinder engine, or as a Model 18, which included the new 65-horsepower V-8. All Model 18s featured a smart V-8 emblem on the center of the headlight bar. The B and 18 were also included as the first digit in the car's vehicle identification number. Behind the engine were a 9-inch diameter clutch and a three-speed manual transmission. Gear ratios were 2.82:1 for first gear, 1.60:1 for second, and 1:1 for third. The standard rear end ratio was 4.11:1.

Thorne Brown mohair was one of the interior materials available on a '32 five-window coupe. The floor covering on Standard coupes was a simple rubber mat. This coupe has been upgraded with a Deluxe-style tapestry carpet.

In 1932 the left taillight was standard and the right light (shown) was optional. Automatic turn signals had yet to be invented.

Early production cars had 4.33:1 rear axles. Ford had been criticized for the Model A's cowl-mounted gas tank. It was deemed dangerous, and passengers were constantly exposed to gasoline fumes. For the 1932 model, the 14-gallon tank was relocated to the rear of the car between the frame rails.

Standard Five-Window Coupe

The five-window coupe was the Standard model. Like all the other Standard models, it was painted entirely black. The body was painted with Pyroxylin lacquer, and the fenders, frame, gas tank, and wheels were dipped and baked with black enamel. For an additional cost, the body and/or wheels could be painted in any of the available 1932 Ford paint schemes. The grille insert on all 1932 Ford passenger cars was painted French Gray.

The five-window coupe seated two comfortably on a full-width (43.5 inches) bench seat. The door openings were rather small, at only 27.8 inches wide, but inside the Standard coupe offered 37 inches of headroom and a

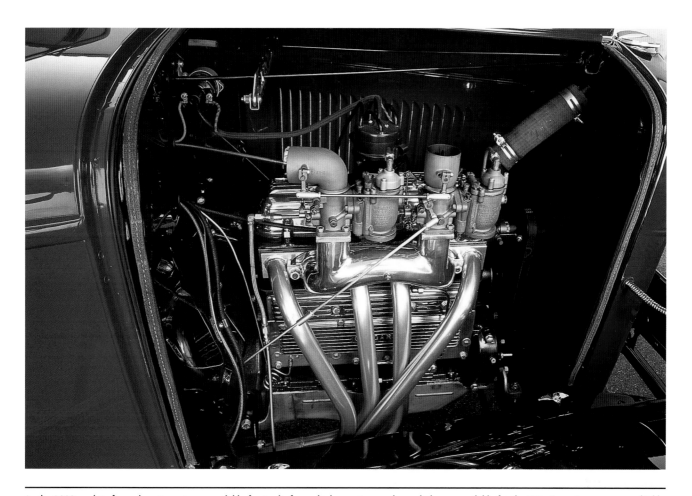

In the 1930s, a lot of speed equipment was available for Ford's four-cylinder engines, and very little was available for the V-8s. Stupar's coupe runs a highly modified Model B engine with a Cragar overhead conversion and a tubular exhaust header. The modifications to Stupar's engine boosted the horsepower from a stock rating of 50 at 2,800 rpm to 86 at 3,200 rpm.

4-Cylinder Engine Specs

BoreXStroke	3.82X4.25	Number of main bearings	3
Cubic inch displacement	195 ci	Pistons	Aluminum alloy
Horsepower	50 at 2,800 rpm	Engine weight with clutch	
Compression ratio	4.6:1	and transmission	464 pounds
Valve arrangement	L in block	Crankcase capacity	5 quarts

Two Winfield downdraft carburetors are mounted on top of a ram's horn aluminum intake manifold. Stupar's modifications to his four-cylinder engine would have allowed it to whip any V-8 in its day.

distance of 18.2 inches from the clutch pedal to the seat. This was more than adequate for any adult in 1932. Added interior appointments included a dome light, sun visors, and a rear window curtain. The interior was upholstered in Diagonal Dash brown mixed cloth or Thorne Brown mohair. The interior window moldings and dash were painted taupe. The only floor covering available on the Standard coupe was a black rubber mat. Safety glass was used in the windshield and was an option for the side and rear windows. The Standard coupe weighed 2,261 pounds with the four-cylinder engine and 2,382 pounds with the V-8. In 1932, a new four-cylinder Model B Standard coupe was priced at $440. The base price for a V-8-powered Model 18 Standard coupe was $490. Total production for the 1932 Standard five-window Ford coupe was 54,107 units.

George Stupar's "Almost" Stock Five-Window

From the outside, George Stupar's coupe looks like a completely stock '32 five-window. It has the optional Medium Maroon paint on the body and wheels, and the optional right-hand taillight. The interior is covered in the original-style brown mohair. When you look closely at this '32 five-window, the subtle modifications make it clear that it is not completely stock.

When Stupar was in high school in 1964, he owned a true 1950s lakes style, Olds-powered five-window. When he sold it in 1980, he came down with a bad case of seller's remorse. The cure was the purchase of this Model B five-window coupe in 1989. It had been stored in a shipping container for over 25 years, and was complete and in excellent shape.

Because of the outstanding condition of this car, Stupar didn't have the heart to cut it up to make a copy of his first '32 coupe. He decided to restore the car to mint condition and do some mild modifications to represent a period-correct, late 1930s-style hot rod. Stupar's magnificent restoration took eight years to complete. The only notable, albeit subtle, exterior modification is the addition of original aftermarket 16-inch diameter Kelsey Hayes bent-spoke wheels. The front tires are 6.00X16, and the rears are 7.00X16, which give the car a gentle rake.

Under the hood, Stupar's coupe sharply deviates from a stock restoration. Instead of installing a modified V-8,

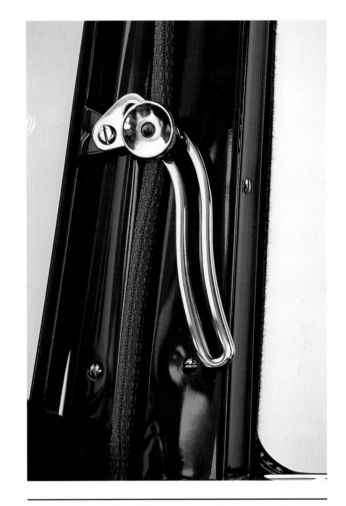

Ventilation was ample in '32 coupes. In addition to a cowl vent, the windshield was hinged at the top and could be tilted out with the help of a pair of windshield swing arms. (Right-hand shown)

V-8 Engine Specs

BoreXStroke	3.06X3.75	Number of main bearings	3
Cubic inch displacement	221 ci	Pistons	Aluminum alloy
Horsepower	65 at 3,400 rpm	Engine weight with clutch	
Compression ratio	5.5:1	and transmission	615 pounds
Valve arrangement	L in block	Crankcase capacity	5 quarts

he chose to hop up the original four-cylinder engine. Using a period-correct Cragar overhead valve conversion, Stupar sharply bumped the horsepower and underhood visual appeal. In addition to the Cragar cylinder head, Stupar added a balanced truck crank, along with a Harman Speed camshaft. The new head increased the compression from the stock ratio of 4.6:1 to a healthy 9:1. Additional engine modifications designed for better lubrication include a modified V-8 oil pump, opened-up oil galleys, and drilled journals. A dual ram's horn-shaped Winfield intake manifold mounts a pair of Winfield carburetors. The exhaust is a four-into-one tubular header that has been Jet Hot-coated. Behind the lightened flywheel is a stock 1932 three-speed that drives into a stock 4:11 rear end. The only modifications made to the chassis were the addition of tubular shocks and the installation of hydraulic brakes.

If the clock were turned back to the late 1930s, Stupar's Model B Standard coupe would be considered a "sleeper." Its benign looks betray its potential for speed. With the overhead conversion, it would have been able to dust off all stock V-8s and give a few of the modified V-8s a run for their money.

Arden Honrud's Unrestored Deluxe Three-WindowCoupe

Ford's top-of-the-line coupe in 1932 was the Deluxe three-window. With the exception of the cowl vent door, all of its Murray-built sheet metal was unique and different from any other '32, including the five-window

Ford's Deluxe coupe in 1932 was this sleek three-window model. Except for the cowl vent, there were no interchangeable body parts between the three-window and five-window coupes. This particular three-window is painted Washington Blue with Tacoma Cream wheels and pin striping, a combination that was available on all Deluxe '32s at no extra cost. Like all other '32 Fords, the fenders were black. This particular coupe is an unrestored original model owned by Ardun Honrud.

All 1932 Fords came with a rear-mounted spare tire. The side fender mounts were optional. This one is equipped with the optional chrome cover. The hubcaps on V-8 models were stamped with a V-8 in the center. Four-cylinder hubcaps had a Ford oval in the center.

As a Deluxe model, the three-window coupe could be ordered at no additional cost in body colors of black, Medium Maroon, Brewster Green, Tunis Gray, Old Chester Gray, Washington Blue, or Winter Leaf Brown. Each of these colors was accented with a harmonizing color for the body reveals, and a third color was used for the pinstripe. Wheels painted in Apple Green, Aurora Red, or Tacoma Cream were also a no-cost option on the Deluxe coupe. As with the Standard coupe, Pyroxylin lacquer was used for the body, and enamel was used for all other exterior components.

coupe. It featured two large 41.8-inch-wide passenger doors that were hinged at the rear for style, and easy entry was a benefit. This rear-hinged door became known as a "suicide door," because if it opened accidentally when the car was in motion, a passenger could be thrown from the vehicle. The Deluxe three-window was the only 1932 Ford model to feature suicide doors, and it was the only one to have front door armrests and a door pull strap. Like the other 1932 Deluxe closed models, the coupe's interior was appointed with a dome light, rear window curtain, glove box, interior sun visors, cigar lighter, ashtray, and attractive tapestry carpet. The dash and interior window frames were painted in a burled woodgrain finish. Upholstery materials included tan broadcloth, Rose Beige mohair, Tan Bedford Cord, or Copra Drab genuine leather. Cowl lights and full safety glass were also standard on the Deluxe coupe.

Three-window '32 coupes were equipped with rear-hinged doors, known as "suicide doors." Honrud's unrestored coupe still has the factory running board cover, which shows wear spots where the original owner pivoted her foot upon entering and exiting her stylish coupe. The area between the body and running board is the exposed frame rail.

Suicide doors swing back to allow easy entry to the coupe's interior. These well-worn Mohair seats on Honrud's coupe were stitched in 1932. Deluxe coupes had a glove box on the dash, and an arm rest and pull strap on the doors. The small T-handle behind the seat is the crank for the rear window.

The cost for a '32 Ford Deluxe coupe with a four-cylinder engine was $500, and the Deluxe coupe with a V-8 was $550. Only 1,258 Deluxe coupes were built as four-cylinder Model Bs, while 22,416 of the V-8 Deluxe coupes were produced. All V-8-equipped cars had a stylish V-8 emblem in the center of the headlight bar and embossed on the hubcaps. Four-cylinder Model B hubcaps featured the Ford script embossed within an oval and a plain headlight bar.

Arden Honrud's Deluxe three-window coupe is an unrestored gem. It was originally purchased on January 28, 1933, at Fortner Motors in Los Angeles. It's one of the late production cars, as evidenced by the 25-louver hood and the dipstick on the driver's side of the V-8 engine. The woman who originally bought the car paid $808.68, which included the cost of a spare tire cover, gas, oil, license, taxes, and insurance. The color is Washington Blue, with Tacoma Cream wheels and striping. Other than the wheels and the grille shell, all of the paint is original. There is even a spot worn through the covering on the driver's side running board, where the owner would pivot her foot, entering or exiting the car. The mohair interior is also original. This three-window "time capsule" is not stashed in a museum or in a trailer. Honrud

Ford used 12 different speedometers during the production run of the '32s. Those used on four-cylinder cars topped out at 80 miles per hour, while the ones used on the V-8 equipped models went up to 90. All gauge panels were machined-turned stainless steel.

occasionally drives the coupe, to the delight of his friends and all those who love '32s.

The big news in 1932 was Ford's new V-8, and while the new Fords were attractive and fast, they had more than their share of teething problems. In the initial design, the idea of a center cross-member for the frame was rejected, so the new frame lacked torsional rigidity. During the nine-month production run, Ford made several attempts to reinforce the frame for stability. Dealers were also instructed to add strengthening plates to the frame. (When the new 1933 Ford was introduced, it would feature the center cross-member that the '32 lacked.)

During the first production year, Ford used three different V-8 blocks. The first 2,000 V-8 engines needed to have their camshafts, pushrods, valves, valve guides, and front covers replaced, and the next 2,000 also had to have the front cover replaced. It wasn't until 1934 that all of the V-8 engine's woes would be fixed.

The efficiency of Ford's basic flathead design, despite bugs in the beginning, was to be proven by a 21-year production lifespan.

In addition to the changes in the frame and engine, there were enough other running changes for those who restore 1932 Fords to divide the production into early, mid-, and late models. For instance, Ford used 12 different speedometers on the 1932 models. Two different hoods were used in domestic production; the early one, with 20 louvers, was used on all Model Bs, and the late one had 25 louvers. It would also be possible to see a Standard five-window coupe with Deluxe items, such as a

The rumble seat on '32 coupes was just wide enough for two adults. The comfortable seat was covered in a simulated leather material. With the rear window rolled down, rumble seat passengers could talk to those in the front seat.

This is the V-8 engine that revolutionized the automobile in 1932. It produced 65 horsepower and was able to push a '32 Ford to 76 miles per hour. The basic flathead design would continue to be installed in Ford passenger cars through 1953.

chromed windshield frame, carpeting, and cowl lights. All 1932 Ford bodies had a reinforcement welded to the inside of the cowl so the cowl lights could be mounted. It was a simple task to drill the holes through the outer skin and attach the lights. A tradition as old as the car itself is the addition of over-the-counter parts to accessorize a new car. Selling cars in the middle of the Depression was tough, and dealers would do almost anything for a sale.

A wide variety of factory and dealer options and accessories could be specified for the 1932 Ford. A side-mounted spare tire moved the spare from the rear to one or both front fenders. With the side-mounted spare, a folding rear trunk rack could be ordered. Ford also provided an optional trunk designed to fit on the rear trunk rack. For an extra $49, a Grigsby-Grunow radio could be added, with the antenna attached to the underside of the drivers side running board. A spotlight, listed as a "sport light," could be added to the drivers side A-pillar. A right-hand side taillight was also available. For those wishing to cover the rear-mounted spare, Ford offered three different spare tire covers.

Up until 1932, Ford's coupes were boxy and limited in performance. With the introduction of the two new coupes and a snappy V-8 in 1932, Ford reestablished itself as the trendsetter for styling and performance in a car for the masses.

Chapter 2

Deuce Coupe Garage

For the past 60 years, backyard garages across the nation have been teeming with hot rod activity. In many of those garages, American skill and ingenuity have been concentrated on '32 deuce coupes. Those fortunate enough to have one of the original deuce coupes have a prize that's coveted by almost everyone in the hot rod world. For the others, a solid fiberglass reproduction of one of the fabled '32 coupes is the basis for a hot rod. Whether it's an original steel car or a quality reproduction, the fun and overall sense of accomplishment of building your own hot rod is as good as it gets.

All it takes to build a deuce coupe is time, energy, space, and money. Once someone decides to build a car, it takes a plan. The plan includes a vision of what the finished product will look like and the finances to fulfill that plan. The vision is important. It determines the theme or look of the finished car—retro, high tech, or something in between. Mixing themes, such as installing billet wheels on a retro rod, is one of the most serious hot rod *faux pas*. A car the builder saw years ago might determine the theme, or it might be a combination of details from the builder's favorite coupes. The theme will ultimately determine the cost. A full-fendered car with a steel body, independent suspension with lots of chrome, and a high-tech engine and transmission will cost more than a retro-styled highboy with a low-buck painted suspension and a junkyard Chevy small-block. One simple rule to remember is that everything will cost exactly double what you thought it would.

The most difficult aspects of building a hot rod involve choices and decisions. When someone builds a '57 Chevy, the choice of grille, bumpers, and taillights is limited and clear-cut. When building a deuce coupe hot rod, however, the choices are unlimited. Most builders stay with traditional themes to avoid creating something dated that will be out of style in 10 years. Those who venture too far outside the lines of hot rod tradition may be unhappy with the results within a

---

Bruce Meyer's garage is every hot rodder's dream—two deuce coupes and a spare flathead engine on a stand. Both '32 three-windows are beautifully detailed highboys. Meyer also has several '32 roadsters and a few historic race cars.

Above: Lucky five-window deuce coupe owner Garry Biddinger wrenches on the old flathead engine that came with his coupe. The original firewall has been butchered, but excellent steel reproductions are available. Biddinger is building this coupe as a daily driver for his wife, Dorothy. It will replace her 1940 Ford pickup.

Right: Biddinger's 1932 five-window looks rough, but it's actually in good shape. The missing lower trunk panel can be easily fabricated, and the surface rust on the rest of the body can be removed. This former hot rod coupe's steel rear fenders have a telltale imprint where '39 teardrop taillights once resided.

matter of years. It's best to look to the cars that have stood the test of time and use what those builders did as a guide.

Finding a Body

A steel deuce coupe body is a hot rodder's Holy Grail. Chasing down an original steel body can be a daunting and expensive proposition. The days of the $100 deuce body are as distant as a low-fat cheeseburger. Today, a decent steel deuce coupe body for under $10,000 is a bargain. You can usually find one for under that amount at most large swap meets, but it will no doubt be freshly primed. This is an excellent indication that the body underneath is less than perfect. In fact, it will probably be filled with body filler and will no doubt be missing many of the hard-to-find interior trim pieces, such as window frames. Cars can be found today that everyone overlooked years ago because they needed extensive repairs or were poorly restored or modified. Correcting a bad restoration will often cost a fortune. That $6,000 bargain '32 coupe body may cost well over $20,000 after the bodywork is complete and

Gibbon is one of the largest suppliers of fiberglass bodies to the hot rodding industry. Here, a '32 three-window body is being assembled on an original '32 frame at the Gibbon shop. A good fiberglass reproduction '32 body cost about half of what a steel body costs.

the missing parts are found. The best advice I ever received was to buy the absolute best body you could afford, because it will be cheaper in the long run.

One way to obtain a complete steel body coupe is to buy an older restoration. This is an excellent, albeit expensive, way to get a solid body with all the trim pieces. Many hot rodders have financed their project by selling off the unneeded components to those who are restoring a similar model. Turning a restoration into a hot rod is also an excellent way to make enemies within the restoration community. Restorers hate to see hot rods evolve from a fully restored car or an original car that is worthy of restoration. Financially, a well-built '32 Ford hot rod will have a higher value than an excellent '32 Ford restoration.

An alternative to a steel deuce body is a fiberglass reproduction. Many purists turn their noses up at the thought of a fiberglass body, but it's an affordable way to get into a deuce coupe. Both three- and five-window body styles are available, with either a chopped or standard height roof. What's nice about ordering a "new" deuce coupe body is that the prospective owner can select

This Gibbon technician is assembling a mold for one of its fiberglass deuce grille shells. An original shell in excellent condition sells for approximately $1,000. A good steel reproduction sells for approximately $210, and a high-quality fiberglass reproduction can be purchased for $125.

from a long list of options. In addition to a chopped top, options include a recessed firewall, hidden door hinges, trunk or rumble seat, roll down or fixed rear window, a filled or working cowl vent, electric windows, and a tilt-out windshield. Most manufacturers of fiberglass deuce coupe bodies will do their best to suit every customer's needs, including chopping an additional inch or two on the roof, or adding a louvered steel deck lid in place of the fiberglass deck lid. Manufacturers can also add working door glass and door latches. Most manufacturers assemble the body on an original '32 frame or jig that is dimensionally accurate. Interiors of the bodies are reinforced with steel, hardwood, or a combination of both. A good fiberglass deuce coupe body can fool an expert into thinking the car is an original steel model. By the time the owner gets ready for paint, the cost of the fiberglass body will be about half of what a steel body will cost.

Another advantage of a fiberglass body is that it can be ordered with a chopped top of a standard dimension (usually 3 inches) at no additional cost. Changing the amount of the chop on a fiberglass body will cost additional money, but it will be far less than the cost of chopping the top on a steel body. Chopping tops on deuce coupes has been a tradition for over 50 years. It was initially done to reduce the amount of wind resistance for the coupes that ran on the dry lakes. Hot rodders also noticed that it improved the proportions of the car. An unchopped deuce coupe tends to look a little top heavy and boxy. When properly chopped, the roof and the body are more harmonious. An automotive designer once told me that the height of the roof should be only one-third of the overall body height. A deuce coupe with the 3-inch chop fits those dimensions perfectly.

John Guilmet has been building hot rods all of his life. This '32 three-window is his latest project. Guilmet fabricated a new lower rear panel, and he is in the process of finishing off the surface. Straight three-window bodies like this one are a rare find.

Chopping and Channeling

Chopping the top on a steel deuce coupe is one of the most distinct changes that can be made to the car, but it's not an easy task. It's a lot like getting a tattoo. Once the top is chopped, it's next to impossible to reverse the process. If it's done poorly, it's difficult to repair. Putting the saw to a 70-year old steel body is not a job for the faint-hearted or the inexperienced. Chopping the top on a '32 coupe is not as simple as cutting a section out and welding it back together again. The windshield posts on both the three- and five-window coupes are laid back at a 10-degree angle, and the rear of the roof tapers slightly toward the top. It's like trying to take a cut out of the center of a funnel. The more that is cut out, the greater is the mismatch. There are two ways of fixing the mismatch. The windshield posts can be leaned back, or the roof can be lengthened. The experienced pros in the chopping business prefer to not lean the windshield posts

Some of the nicest hot rods come out of the So-Cal Speed Shop in Pomona, California. This chopped '32 five-window is being built for a customer. The steel body on this coupe is about as perfect as one can find.

back to solve the problem. Leaning the posts back creates an uneven surface for the windshield, resulting in a windshield that won't properly seal. The other alternative requires the roof to be stretched by the addition of a small panel to fill in the gap created by the front half of the roof that was moved forward and the back half that was moved rearward.

Before the first cut is made on a deuce coupe's top, a set of parallel cut lines must be scribed onto the surface of the roof and across the doors. These lines must be accurate, because a mistake of as little as 1/16 inch will be noticeable. In addition, the cut line must be stepped up to cut as close to the center of the rear window as possible, because the rear window is slightly higher than the door windows. The doors must fit properly before the sheet metal is cut, because fitting doors afterward is a nightmare. A power saw is used to cut the sheet metal, approximately 1/4 inch away from the line. Tin snips are used to get to the scribed line, and then the area is dressed with a sanding disc. A 3-inch chop in a '32 coupe will require the roof to be stretched 0.62 inch. This is done in an area over the door, where the section shape is relatively constant. This also means that the door frames must be stretched. It's critical that the door frames be straight so the door glass can travel up and down smoothly. Vertical slits are made in the A pillars and the rear of the roof so the surfaces can be aligned.

The process of dropping the body down over the frame rails is called "channeling." This five-window coupe has been channeled approximately 5 inches. (A '32's frame rail is 6 inches wide.) The typical channel is 6 inches, the width of the frame rail. Channeling gives the vehicle a lower profile without sacrificing ride and handling.

When chopping a '32 five-window coupe, the cut line is located above the upper door hinge. A three-window coupe has three door hinges, two on the body and one on the roof. To simplify the amount of work to be done when chopping a three-window, many will remove the upper hinge. Experienced customizers will keep that upper hinge.

Once the top is tack-welded together and the alignment is correct, it will be fully welded. The interior window moldings must also be cut and welded back together. The next task is to cut the windshield frame. A '32 windshield frame consists of an upper section that is U-shaped, and a lower section with a mitered corner where the two sections join. To cut the frame, cut the lower ends of the upper section and bolt the two pieces back together with new glass. The glass is flat on a '32, so replacing a windshield, or side or rear window is easy.

Channeling is another hot rod trick used to lower a deuce coupe. In the 1950s, channeling was very popular

Looking at the surface of this roof, it's hard to believe that it's been chopped. Expert metal finishing has eliminated the need for body filler. The roof has not been filled, so the wooden support structure for the fabric insert is visible.

on the East Coast and in the Midwest. A channeled car is one on which the body is lowered over the frame rails. On a '32, the body is customarily dropped 6 inches, because that is the width of the frame rail. A 6-inch drop is the most pleasing to the eye, because the bottom of the frame rail is in alignment with the bottom edge of the body. Channeling is easier than chopping a top, but it usually left to an experienced metal worker. When a car is channeled, the body is cut away from the floor. The body is then dropped down over the floor and frame rails and is reattached to the body. The rear frame rails must be cut to fit within the rear deck, and the firewall must also be cut to allow clearance for the frame rails. Chopping and channeling gets a '32 coupe about as low as possible. The only drawback is the lack of headroom.

Two other body modifications common to a '32 coupe are recessing the firewall and filling in the opening in the roof. Recessing the firewall entails moving the firewall rearward 2 to 3 inches. This is done to provide clearance for an overhead valve V-8, most of which have the distributor in the rear of the engine. A flathead-powered '32 can keep the original firewall location, because the engine is shorter than most overhead valve engines and its distributor is in the front of the engine. To fill in the opening in the roof and make it look correct, the panel that fills in the opening cannot be a simple, flat sheet metal insert. The panel must have a slight crown, or gentle curve, to blend with the natural curves of the roof. Many hot rodders will search junkyards for a station wagon roof as a starting point. An accomplished sheet metal worker can make a crowned panel from flat stock to fill in the opening. When a fiberglass deuce coupe body is ordered today, a recessed firewall is a no-cost option, and all fiberglass bodies come with a filled roof.

Interior

The inside of a '32 Ford coupe is cramped. Climbing into one that has been chopped, especially a five-window,

can be difficult. Suicide doors on the three-window makes entry easier, but anyone over 6 feet tall must make a few adjustments to drive in comfort. There was a sizable package tray in factory models between the seat and the rear window. Eliminating this tray gives the occupants an additional 6 inches of legroom. All '32 coupes were equipped with a comfortable bench seat from the

In this shot of the interior of the chopped five-window, the cut lines in the roof's sheet metal are barely visible. The wood around the windows provides a tack strip for interior trim.

factory. Most deuce coupe builders follow tradition and use the original bench seat or install one of the many aftermarket bench seats available. Leather, vinyl, and tweed cloth are the most popular upholstery materials.

One of the ways to create more interior space is to install a tilt steering column. Builders either modify a junkyard column or buy one of the many aftermarket tilt columns. Installing a smaller steering wheel is another way of gaining more entry room. The most popular steering wheel in retro rods is the Bell three- or four-spoke sprint car-style wheels.

The list of deuce coupe creature comforts reads like an option list on a new luxury car. Today's deuce coupe owner can drive from coast to coast in air-conditioned comfort, with cruise control and a wide variety of AM/FM radios, tape players, and CD changers.

Rick Cronin, in red shirt, is a retired General Motors engineer who has been a gearhead all his life. His latest project is a '32 three-window coupe. The chassis is almost complete. The chopped body has been media-blasted, and a new recessed firewall has been installed.

Chassis

Once the body has been selected, it has to sit on a frame. Deuce rails are the only frames that look good under a '32 coupe body. The '32 frame rails have the characteristic "beauty mark" along the side that gives them a distinctive look. That beauty mark adds character to a '32 highboy. To be used for a hot rod, the original rails must be reinforced. This can be done by boxing, or welding a plate to the open inside of the C-section rail. For additional strength, a new center K-member is usually added. Many aftermarket manufacturers are making reproduction rails and complete chassis because of the popularity of the '32 frame. Everything from a bare frame to a complete chassis with independent front and rear suspension can be ordered. These chassis are categorized as Stage I, Stage II, and Stage III. A Stage I chassis is usually a bare set of rails with cross-members installed. A Stage II chassis includes the frame with mounts for the engine, master cylinder, and pedals added. A Stage III chassis is complete with steering box, springs, shocks, axles, brakes, and is ready to mount a body and install an engine. There's so much to say regarding hot rod chassis that several books have been written about them. Today's reproduction chassis are well engineered and safer than ever—a great foundation for any deuce coupe.

Tires and Wheels

Tires and wheels can make or break any car, especially a deuce coupe. The traditional look since the 1940s has been "big 'n' littles"—large tires in the rear and small ones in front. Dry lakes racers were the first to put larger rear tires on their cars, to effectively change the rear end gear ratio for a higher top speed. The larger rear tires fit within the deuce's rear fenders, and when run without fenders, it worked well with the proportions of the body. The look remains the same 50 years later.

Today hot rodders are using a wide mix of tires and wheels on deuce coupes. Car enthusiasts who are firmly rooted in the past lean toward bias-ply tires, but they

have a wide variety of radials to choose from, including wide whitewalls. Before the advent of mag wheels, all that was available for hot rodders were wire wheels or standard steel wheels with hubcaps. The big 'n' little tire arrangement required wider wheels in the rear to accommodate the larger tires, and the trend in wheel size has followed the tire trend. Front tires that are too small and rear tires that are too big will tend to make a car look cartoonish. If they are both the same size, it will make the

Because of its simplicity, building a '32 Ford is relatively easy. With the body off of the frame, all of the engine and chassis components can be easily reached. This original set of frame rails has been boxed, and new cross-members have been added. The engine, transmission, gas tank, and full exhaust system have also been installed.

front of the car look heavy. There is no mathematical formula for sizing tires and wheels to a hot rod. The combination of chassis, wheels, and tires develop the car's "stance." Stance creates the car's attitude. When the stance is right, the attitude is right.

Engine and Transmission

In the 1940s and early 1950s, there was only one choice for a hot rod engine—the Ford flathead. It had evolved into a great powerplant and a lot of speed equipment was available. Not long after the first overhead V-8s were in production, they found their way in between a set of deuce rails. By the late 1950s, only the diehards were running flatheads. The new small-block Chevy was a perfect fit under a deuce hood; it performed well, and it was reliable and inexpensive. So long, flathead.

A wave of nostalgia has hit today's hot rod builder, and flatheads are cool once again. Parts are plentiful and modern engine building techniques have been applied to an engine whose production ended in 1953. Today's flathead is not as powerful as an overhead V-8, but it is reliable and just about the best-looking engine to ever sit in a deuce coupe's engine bay. It also has a sound that cannot be imitated.

The engine in Cronin's coupe is a small-block Chevy with a Corvette dual-four-barrel setup. The exhaust headers are rare set of Fenton cast-iron manifolds. Cronin has installed a four-speed transmission behind the Chevy engine.

Small-block Chevy engines have long been a favorite of hot rodders. They are the least expensive of all the modern V-8s because of the millions of engines that Chevrolet built. Dollar for dollar, it's easier to squeeze additional horsepower from a small-block Chevy than any other engines. Other hot rod favorites include any late 1950s and early 1960s Olds, Cadillac, Pontiac, or Buick V-8. In their day, these and the small-block Chevys, were the engines of choice for hot rods. Plenty of vintage speed equipment for these engines is available at swap meets, and some of the equipment is still manufactured today.

A wide array of V-8 engines can be bought in a box from the parts counter of your nearest new car dealership. These "crate engines" can be less expensive than rebuilding an old engine. They can also be purchased with more tire-smoking power than will ever be needed for a street coupe. With the exception of the Chrysler Hemi, all of these engines will fit under the unmodified hood of a '32 Ford.

There was a time when stick shift transmissions were the only kind of gearboxes available, and a '39 Ford transmission with Lincoln Zephyr gears was about the best gearbox anyone could have in a hot rod. In the 1960s, transmission technology took some giant leaps, due to the musclecar craze. The three- and four-speed manual transmissions that were being produced were stronger than ever. In the 1950s and early 1960s, an automatic transmission in a hot rod would have gotten the owner laughed off the street, but in the mid- and late 1960s, new automatic transmissions were being introduced that were stronger and more efficient. The energy crisis in the 1970s sent transmission designers back to the drawing board to create a new generation of

One of the most gratifying aspects of building a deuce coupe is inviting friends over to help. Here, the owner (yours truly) is taking a break, while his buddy (fellow MBI author Dan Burger) wrenches on the engine.

Look what I found in the workshop behind Don Garlits' Museum of Drag Racing! It's Don's personal '32 three-window under construction. Like most drag racers, Garlits was a hot rodder before he hit the strip.

The rake on Bruce Meyer's three-window is perfect. Correct body proportions, a well-designed chassis, and the proper big 'n' little tire combination make a great stance. One rule of thumb is to have the rear tires fit within the body's rear wheel opening and be concentric with the arc of the wheel house reveal.

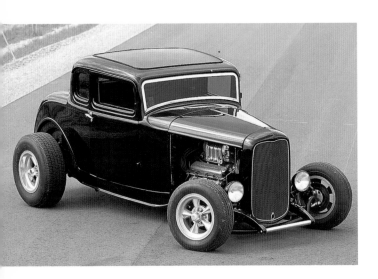

The nose-down attitude on Elwood Peterson's black steel-bodied '32 five-window is achieved through a 5-inch dropped front axle and properly sized tires on American Mag wheels. The hood sides have been left off so everyone can see the blown small-block Chevy engine.

John Bade's '32 five-window was hot rodded in the 1950s. At that time the owner, in an effort to upgrade the ride and handling, installed the front and rear suspension from a 1956 Chevy. The front fenders have had blisters molded into the surfaces to provide clearance for the upper control arms.

The smiling man behind the wheel is Aaron Kahan. He owns this Buick nailhead-powered '32 five-window. Early Buick V-8s were one of the popular overhead valve engines in the late 1950s and early 1960s that were stuffed between deuce frame rails. Kahan is a member of the Choppers hot rod club of Burbank, California. This is one of a growing number of clubs devoted to preserving hot rodding's roots by building and driving traditional hot rods.

Left: The engine choice for a deuce coupe is subjective. Traditionalists like flatheads because they were the first hot rod V-8s, and others like small-block Chevys, because of their simplicity and low cost. This '32 coupe is being built with a vintage Chrysler Hemi, which requires a slightly recessed firewall. The Hilborn injection unit has been converted to electronic fuel injection. This hot rod will have the look of the 1950s with the drivability of a new luxury car.

Below: Flathead engines will always have a certain mystique in the hot rodding world. It was the first low-cost V-8 and therefore the first V-8 to be hot rodded. They were quickly replaced when overhead valve engines became popular in the 1950s. Today, many deuce coupe builders have returned to Ford's original V-8. A full-race flathead with three Stromberg carburetors on top is barely visible behind the front tire on Richard Lux's five-window.

Above: The itch to get into your deuce coupe and drive it is more than some owners can stand. Bill Webb's '32 three-window is far from finished, but it is drivable. It will eventually have a full set of fenders, and once the bodywork is completed, it will be painted black.

Left: Brent Bell's superstraight black '32 five-window has been built in a traditional style. It rolls on 16-inch steel wheels with small hubcaps. Bell has opted for a set of 1932 California license plates. Other details of note are a painted windshield frame, stylish curved headlight mounts with original '32 headlights, and a small "peep" mirror on the door.

highly efficient overdrive automatic and manual transmissions. Today, most hot rods are being built with these overdrive automatic transmissions, but there are a few diehards who will always feel that a real hot rod should have a manual transmission.

Details

Details make the difference between a deuce coupe that has been thrown together and one that has been carefully planned. The aftermarket is rife with traditional and billet accessories that blend well with the style of any coupe. Manufacturers offer several traditional choices for rearview mirrors, headlight mounts, and taillights on a deuce coupe. Accessories must blend harmoniously with the car's style. A bad choice will stand out like a pimple on a supermodel's nose. Hot rodders use the word "sano," a derivative of sanitary, to describe a car that has the right look. Correct body proportions, the

Jeff Vodden's chopped and channeled three-window is powered by a flathead. Holes in the quarter-panel reveal where the fenders once resided. Vodden and many other traditional hot rodders have turned back the clock by building and driving real hot rods, just the way they did in the 1950s.

right stance, and the many little details that round out the car characterize that look.

Hittin' the Road

Don Garlits once said of the hot rods of the 1950s, "When it runs, it's done!" Driving a deuce coupe, even if it's in primer or the interior isn't fully trimmed, is the best part of owning one. Most hot rods of the 1940s and 1950s were a challenge to drive, due to a poorly engineered chassis and marginal tires. They would dart from side to side, and they rode rough. Today's deuce chassis feature revised steering systems that eliminate bump steer and Panhard bars to reduce side-to-side sway. Today's reproduction bias-ply tires are a vast improvement over the tires of the 1950s and 1960s. These developments, with all the advances in engine and transmission technology, make driving a deuce one of the most fun things anyone can do.

Having a big blown Hemi engine doesn't stop Bob Berry, owner of this three-window, from racking up a lot of miles. Cars are made to be driven, and no car is more fun to drive than a deuce coupe.

Chapter 3

Five-Window Deuce Coupe Hot Rods

"Where were you in '62?" was the question that was asked in the promotional material for *American Graffiti*, a low-budget movie released in August 1973 that became one of America's landmark films. The subject was the cruising culture of the American streets, and the star of the show was a yellow five-window deuce coupe. *American Graffiti* showcased a number of actors whose future careers in films and television would become legendary, including Harrison Ford, Ron Howard, and Richard Dreyfuss.

American Graffiti was the dream come true of producer Gary Kurtz and George Lucas. Both were heavily involved in the selection of the cars that represented the

era. The '32 coupe was found in the Los Angeles area for $1,300. Kurtz was drawn to the coupe because of its chopped top. The car was full fendered and had been hot rodded, but to fulfill its movie role, it needed some extensive work. The film's transportation manager, Henry Travers, guided the car's transformation. Lucas' vision included bobbed rear fenders, motorcycle front fenders, and a chopped grille shell. The coupe was stripped of several coats of paint, and a fresh coat of Canary Yellow lacquer was added. The entire front end was chrome-plated and a fresh small-block Chevy engine was added. The engine had a Man-A-Fre intake with four Rochester two-barrel carburetors. Lucas also wanted a set of sprint car-style headers. The red and white interior was dyed black, and a pocket was added to the right door for the scene in which the coupe's driver, John Milner, (played by Paul LeMat) received a ticket for not having a license plate light. The frame was modified for removable platforms that would hold a camera, sound equipment, and as many as four production staff members to film the scenes set inside the car.

The '32 coupe used in *American Graffiti* was originally a full-fendered hot rod. The front fenders were stripped off, the rear fenders were bobbed, and a fresh coat of yellow paint was added. Like most movie cars, it has a few rough edges that are part of its charm and authenticity. Present owner Rick Figari maintains its drivability, but refuses to restore the car.

A pair of motorcycle front fenders were added to the *American Graffiti* coupe for early 1960s authenticity. It was during that time period that police would hassle hot rodders for not having fenders on their cars. Small motorcycle fenders became a popular addition. George Lucas requested the sprint car-style headers to give the car a more aggressive look.

Along with the '32 coupe, the staff had to prepare three other cars for the movie: a '58 Impala, a '55 Chevy, and the Pharaoh's chopped '51 Mercury. Today, when a movie or television series is made, several duplicate cars are available in case one fails, but the only duplicate car in *American Graffiti* was a second '55 Chevy for the rollover scene. One of the other challenges in the movie was to get actor Paul LeMat comfortable driving the coupe. He had to look as if he'd grown up in the car. LeMat drove in every scene except the final one, when the coupe and '55 Chevy raced on Paradise Road. Travers took the wheel for that one.

After the filming, Universal Studios felt that the movie would surely bomb and decided to sell off all of the rolling stock to recoup some of its investment. The coupe was put up for sale for $1,500 with no takers. The '58 Impala sold for $200. Universal decided to hang onto the coupe and leave it where sightseers on the studio's back lot tour could see it. Its engine and instrument panel were used for detail shots in another cult hot rod classic, *The California Kid*. The unexpected success of *American Graffiti* made those at Universal who decided to keep the coupe look like visionaries. The yellow '32 was dusted off, repainted, and

Above: Powering the *American Graffiti* coupe is a small-block Chevy with a Man-A-Fre four-carb intake. The engine was built more for its visual appeal than for horsepower. Twin master cylinders on the firewall control the brakes and hydraulic clutch.

Left: The *American Graffiti* coupe's interior remains the same as it was when the movie was filmed. The tuck 'n' roll seats were dyed black for the movie, but today some of the original red color is showing through. A pocket and some chrome trim were added to the passenger side door for the "ticket" scene. ("File that under 'CS.'") The famous piston gearshift knob is on the Hurst shifter.

The *American Graffiti* coupe's grille shell was chopped, and the front suspension was chromed for the movie. When the car was initially purchased for the production, the top had been chopped. When current owner Figari bought the coupe, the original movie prop license plates were in the trunk. The license plate, THX 138, refers to George Lucas' 1971 cult classic film, *THX-1138*.

rechromed for the sequel, *More American Graffiti*. Unfortunately, the sequel, like most sequels, failed to live up to its expectations. The coupe went up for sale in a sealed auction bid. The winner was Steve Fitch, who also owned the black '55 Chevy from the movie.

In 1985, Fitch sold the car to Rick Figari. When Figari first saw the movie, he was only eight years old. It was love at first sight for Figari, but he would have to wait 12 years before he could take possession. Figari's

first task was to make the coupe roadworthy, and he drove it a lot for the first few years. As Figari began to appreciate the historical significance of the coupe, he limited the driving and made the car available for shows across the nation. He even has his own website (www.milnerscoupe.com) devoted to the car.

It's gratifying to see that the most famous of all five-window coupes lives on. It's especially nice to know that the insidious bug of overrestoration hasn't

Alex "Axle" Idzardi's '32 coupe was built in the style of the 1960s. It takes many of its visual cues from Clarence Catallo's original blue three-window coupe, the original *Little Deuce Coupe*. These features include metallic blue paint, a chopped top with a white insert, and wide whitewall tires on chrome wheels.

The interior of Idzardi's coupe is trimmed in white and blue metalflake vinyl. Even the steering wheel and knob on the Hurst shifter are blue metalflake.

bitten Figari. The coupe's rough edges are still there, worn like a badge of honor.

Sparky's Black Coupe

Another five-window that was bought around the time *American Graffiti* was in production is owned by Mike "Sparky" Sparks of Glendora, California. Sparky bought the car in 1971 for $500. The man he purchased it from had owned it since 1952 and had driven it only twice since 1953. Sparky made the car roadworthy and drove it until November 1978, when he decided to rebuild the entire car. Like many car projects, this one sat until 1995, when Sparky's friends motivated him to put it together. In November 1999, Sparky drove his almost-completed coupe for the first time in 21 years. It lacked upholstery, a top insert, and hood, but it was roadworthy. In January 2000, Sparky trailered it to Howard's upholstery shop in Lake Havasu, Arizona, and in March, he drove it home to Southern California.

Sparky's five-window is powered by a stock Chevy 350 engine. The only upgrade is the Edelbrock aluminum intake with a 650 Holley carb. Behind the engine is a stock Turbohydro 400. The frame is an original Ford chassis that has been fully boxed and upgraded with a 9-inch Ford rear end and a dropped front axle. B.F. Goodrich radials are mounted on 1950s-era 15X7 wire wheels that are painted apple green.

Axle's No-Frills Five-Window

One deuce coupe owner who was heavily influenced by Chili Catallo's famous three-window was Alex "Axle" Idzardi. He wanted to build a '32 coupe that had the look of an early 1960s hot rod with the flavor of Catallo's *Little Deuce Coupe*. Idzardi is also president of the *Shifters* car club. The *Shifters* is the first of the clubs dedicated to preserving America's true hot rod culture. Their cars are rough by today's spit-shined standards, but are typical of the average hot rod that roamed the streets in the 1950s and 1960s. Their home-built simplicity and the lack of

From the rear, the nose-down rake on Idzardi's coupe is quite apparent. On the rear are 1953 Buick taillights, a vintage gold California license plate, and a *Shifters* club plaque.

Powering Idzardi's coupe is a 1960s era tripower Pontiac engine, complete with a chromed generator. The headers were custom made and painted white.

catalog-ordered billet aluminum components are a big part of their charm.

Idzardi's '32 coupe, like the cars of his fellow *Shifters* club members, is based on an original Ford steel body. It has been chopped approximately 4 inches. The only other body modification is a filled cowl, which was a

popular modification in the 1950s and 1960s. On the rear is a pair of 1953 Buick taillights and a *Shifters* club plaque. The metallic blue paint and white top insert pay homage to Catallo's coupe. Another early hot rodding trick Idzardi employed on his coupe was to paint the firewall white. In the 1950s, white paint was a low-cost

Sam Davis' '32 five-window was designed to look as if it had just rolled out of a 1940s hot rod time capsule. Back then, cars were built from spare parts and were driven with or without paint. Davis' coupe has been on the covers of both *Hot Rod* and *Rod & Custom* magazines.

substitute for chrome plating. Chrome is apparent on the front suspension, which features a dropped front axle and reversed eyes on the spring. The frame is fully boxed, and a Model A front cross-member helps lower the front end. Big 'n' little bias-ply whitewalls ride on 15X6-inch chrome wheels.

In keeping with the 1960s theme, Idzardi installed a tripower Pontiac engine backed by a Muncie four-speed transmission. The headers were handmade, and pipes from the collectors tuck under the frame to a pair of mufflers for street use. To maintain the retro theme, a generator was installed instead of an alternator. A pair

The top on Davis' coupe has been chopped a little over 2 1/2 inches, and the deck lid has been louvered. A 1940 Ford rear axle is equipped with a Halibrand quick-change center section. The taillights are 1939 Ford teardrop with blue dots.

of vintage Moon finned aluminum valve covers and a trio of chrome air cleaners top off the carpet.

The retro look continues inside, where pearl white and metalflake blue vinyl covers the bench seat. On top of the Izardi-built column is an NOS blue metalflake Ansen steering wheel. A Hurst shifter emerges from the blue-speckled engine. A fellow *Shifters* member donated a pair of 1960-era NOS clear blue metalflake floormats.

Idzardi and his fellow *Shifters* have started a trend in home-built no-frills cars. His '32 is constantly being worked on and enhanced, but it's also being driven as much as possible. To Idzardi and the *Shifters*, having fun means driving their cars and hanging out with their buddies. Idzardi's coupe harkens back to a day when ingenuity and hard work took the place of a Visa Gold card.

Sam Davis' Primer Five-Window

Sam Davis' '32 five-window also has a retro look. It also has the distinct honor of being on the covers of *Hot Rod* and *Rod & Custom* magazines. What's even more amazing is that his car is painted in flat black primer. These prestigious magazines know quality and style, and that's what Davis' coupe is all about.

While Davis was growing up in Southern California, the hot rodding bug didn't bite him until after he got drag racing out of his system. He first built a Junior Fuel dragster and then graduated to a Top Fuel dragster. His most famous ride was the twin-Chevy-engined *Freight Train*. In that car he won the gas portion of the U.S. Fuel and Gas Championship at Famoso Drag Strip in Bakersfield, California, where he ran a top speed of 207 miles per hour. After the drags, Davis' interest turned to European sports cars, but the road eventually led back to hot rods. "After going to the L.A. Roadster show for 20-plus years, it dawned on me that a hot rod of my own was what I needed," says Davis.

The car of Davis' vision was a 1940s-style coupe. In 1991, he started by gathering as many original parts as he

The red vinyl interior blends well with the red wheels and red grille insert on Davis' five-window. The shifter is attached to a '39 Ford transmission. An unpretentious rubber mat covers the floor.

Adhering to the 1940s theme, Davis selected a Ford flathead for power. Period-perfect speed equipment includes Navarro heads, a Mallory ignition, and a Thickston intake manifold with two Stromberg 97 carburetors. On the firewall is a beehive oil filter. A small alternator is hidden inside the original generator.

could find and afford. Some of the pieces he found were unusual and rare. For the engine, he found a Thickstun PM-7 dual carb intake; for the interior he located a rearview mirror with a clock, and a shift knob with an inset thermometer. Added to the chassis is a 1940 Ford rear axle with a Halibrand quick-change center. Other

swap meet discoveries include a pair of 1932 California license plates and four 16-inch-diameter Kelsey-Hayes wire wheels. Firestone bias-ply tires, 5.50s in front and 7.00s in the rear, are mounted on the wheels.

With the help of Scott Gildner, Davis chopped the top 2.6 inches. He also removed the drip rails and filled

Michael "Sparky" Sparks' '32 five-window appears to have been dipped in black lacquer. Apple Green wire wheels were an option on the original '32s, and the color combination still looks good today. The low front end is achieved through a combination of a dropped front axle, a Model A cross-member, and 195x60R15 tires. The only modification that was made to the body of Sparks' five-window is a filled grille shell and an added bull-nose trim piece. The stock headlight bar was replaced with a dropped version. Smaller-than-stock, 7-inch Deitz headlights were added.

the grille shell. Gildner added louvers to the deck lid and hood top panels. In addition to all that work, he filled a few bullet holes and then sprayed on the Dupont DP-90 black primer. The wheels and grille insert were painted bright red, with a matching shade of red vinyl covering the interior.

The only logical choice for the engine of a 1940s-era deuce coupe is the fabled Ford flathead. Davis' engine is a 1948 vintage with a 239-ci displacement. It runs a Winfield cam, Mallory distributor, and Navarro aluminum heads. The two Stromberg 97s that provide the fuel are topped with angle-cut chrome velocity

Stock '32 Ford taillights leave a lot to be desired. Sparks reduced the chances of having his five-window rear-ended when he added a strip of LEDs between the gas tank and lower body. They remain hidden in the shadows, and are visible only when illuminated.

stacks. Backing the engine is a '39 Ford transmission with Lincoln Zephyr gears. Davis does not like the unreliability of generators. An alternator is the best solution, but it doesn't fit the style of his car. Davis' ingenious solution was to hollow out the inside of the stock generator and slip in a Mitsubishi alternator. The result is 12 volts of reliable power and the correct look.

When asked to state the primary use of his deuce coupe, Davis simply said, "Fun." In addition to driving the wheels off this five-window, he's been on the River City Reliability Run, has taken it to the Antique National Drags, and has push-started a vintage Top Fuel dragster at the NHRA California Hot Rod Reunion. "I've drag raced, road raced, and ridden dirt

Above: Powering Sparks' coupe is a stock Chevy 350. The only modifications are the aluminum intake manifold and Holley carb. Valve covers are polished Corvette units and the Chevy ram's horn exhaust manifolds have been ground smooth and coated.

Right: Too many additions would have detracted from the simple beauty of Henry Ford's original design. A rearview mirror is a necessity for a car that is driven as much as Michael Sparks' coupe. Because of its smoothly curved shape, this rear view mirror is called a "swan neck."

Above: Shaun Price is the third owner of this '32 five-window. The body is all stock and all steel. The only modification is the dropped headlight bar.

Left: The interior of Sparks' coupe is trimmed in black Mercedes vinyl. Sparks built the steering column from 1 3/4-inch-diameter exhaust tubing. It's topped with a three-spoke Bell steering wheel. Stock window crank handles actuate switches for the electric windows. An air conditioner and CD changer are hidden between the seat back and trunk.

bikes, and I have a pilot's license," confides Davis. "But this car was gratifying to build and the most fun I've had with anything mechanical ever."

Shaun Price's Full-Fendered Five Window

Shaun Price takes the same approach to his '32 five-window as Davis—fun. Price's car was built to be a driver, and in the five years he's owned it, he has put on over 40,000 miles. Price is the third owner. The previous owner of his coupe had it for 35 years.

Above: The low stance on Shaun Price's '32 is due to big 'n' little tires and a 5-inch dropped front axle. In the five years that Price has owned the coupe, he's put over 40,000 miles on it. Air conditioning, leather seats, and a CD changer are comfort perks that have been added to Price's coupe.

Left: Part of Price's formula to make his coupe a solid driver was to install a simple engine. Other than a little chrome, the 305-ci Chevy engine in his coupe is unmodified. The small black cylinder on the firewall is the cruise-control module.

Originally built into a hot rod in the 1950s and then rebuilt in the mid-1970s, shortly after the film *American Graffiti* was released, John McClintock's '32 five-window has many of the features of the movie's famous coupe. Deviations include a body color frame, an unchopped grille shell, mag wheels, and a front-mounted Moon tank.

Price's all-steel rumble seat coupe is full fendered and very red. With the exception of the dropped headlight bar, the body is completely stock from bumper to bumper. Original accessory cowl lights have been, added along with a chromed windshield frame and second taillight. The car's noticeable rake is the result of a 5-inch dropped front axle and big 'n' little Michelin radials on 15-inch steel wheels. The rear axle is an 8-inch unit out of a Ford Maverick. Mustang disc brakes are in the front, with drums in the rear.

Price selected a 305-ci small-block Chevy engine to power his coupe. The only modifications are chromed Corvette valve covers and an aftermarket air cleaner. The transmission is a Turbo 400, which is also unmodified. Stainless exhaust pipes lead into a pair of Turbo mufflers for that hot rod sound.

While Price retained the factory cowl vent, he opted for air conditioning in his deuce coupe because of the number of miles he clocks and because he lives in Arizona. Adding to the driving comfort is an interior

69

In the 1950s, a Southern California high school auto shop class chopped the top and rolled the rear pan on McClintock's coupe. The taillights are from a 1941 Chevy with blue dots. Small nerf bars (bumpers), also made in the 1950s, are used on the front and rear.

trimmed in gray leather with a gray wool carpet. A LeCarra banjo steering wheel tops a tilt column, and a Pioneer AM/FM radio is wired to a CD changer for those special "road tunes." If that's not enough, Price has even added cruise control.

John McClintock's Yellow Five-Window Highboy

At first glance, John McClintock's '32 coupe looks exactly like the one John Milner used to cruise the streets in *American Graffiti*. It's a chopped yellow highboy with a Chevy engine, but McClintock's coupe first took shape long before the movie was made. When it was rebuilt in the 1970s, some of the flavor of Milner's car from movie was incorporated.

The furthest back McClintock could trace his car's history was to 1952, when it was a class project car for a Southern California high school auto shop. All the body modifications, including the chopped top and rolled rear pan, were done in that class between 1952 and 1954. It was also during that time that the black pleated Naugahyde interior was installed. In the late 1950s it was on the streets, full fendered and running an Olds 303-ci engine. In subsequent years, it changed hands several times, and it ended up in Michigan with brothers Craig and Bryan Smith in the late 1960s. In the early 1970s, they transformed the coupe to the state it's in today. There are some obvious influences from the *American Graffiti* coupe that can be seen, such as the color and multicarbed Chevy V-8. Since 1976, McClintock's coupe remains almost unchanged.

One of the unique aspects of McClintock's coupe is the piece of dark blue-tinted plexiglass used to fill the opening in the roof. It offers additional headroom, and the ability to see the sky. Another interesting interior feature is the chrome-plated dash panel with a woodgrain insert. One of the outstanding features, dripping with nostalgia, is the coupe's 327 Chevy engine. A vintage Edelbrock six-deuce intake manifold mounting Stromberg carbs tops the engine. The valve covers are also vintage Edelbrock with Moon breathers. Other vintage features to note are the nerf bars, front-mounted Moon tank, and Clay Smith "Mr. Horsepower" decals on the sides of the cowl.

The world of five-window deuce coupes is varied. Some are full fendered and others are stripped down highboys. Some use the latest in technology and others rely on time-proven engineering and vintage components. One thing they all have in common is that they're unmistakably cool and a blast to drive.

When McClintock's coupe was rebuilt in the 1970s, a 350-ci small-block replaced the car's vintage Olds engine. Edelbrock valve covers and a six-deuce intake were added. A polished firewall was very popular in the 1950s.

Chapter 4

Three-Window Deuce Coupe Hot Rods

In July 1961, *Hot Rod* magazine's cover car was a hot rod that redefined the way people looked at and built 1932 Ford coupes. That car was Clarence "Chili" Catallo's chopped and channeled three-window. It would soon become known as the *Little Deuce Coupe,* after it appeared on the cover of the Beach Boys record album of the same name. It was a car that evolved from a street-driven hot rod to one of America's premiere show cars.

In 1955, 15-year old Clarence Catallo worked at his parents' small grocery store in Allen Park, a blue-collar suburb of Detroit. In a gas station across from the store, he found a '32 three-window coupe for $75. He had a friend drive it home for him because he was too young to drive it himself. By the time Catallo got his license, the deuce was ready for the street. Initially, the car was

Mike Martin's yellow '32 three-window highboy was constructed to look as if it were built in the mid-1960s. Martin used one of Ford's rare single overhead cam (SOHC)427s for the engine. Steve Davis, one of the West Coast's top car builders, and several of Martin's friends, helped with the car's construction.

channeled, painted dark blue, and powered by a carbureted Olds. It had whitewall tires (dual whites in front) with black wheels and no hubcaps. Catallo took it to the newly opened Detroit Dragway and turned the quarter-mile in 12.9 seconds at 112 miles per hour. Like all hot rods in the 1950s, Catallo's coupe was constantly being changed, and he added more chrome with each version. One of the subtle touches added to the body was the raised rear wheel opening line. This seemingly insignificant feature made the bodyline follow the shape of the rear tire to create a smoother line.

The carbs soon made way for a McCulloch supercharger. Silver scallops were added along with chrome wheels. Catallo, who by now had picked up the nickname "Chili," as in "cool," took the car to Detroit's top customizers, the Alexander Brothers (Mike and Larry). They sectioned the channeled body and added three horizontal wings to each frame rail. They added a custom nose with vertically stacked quad headlights, and reworked the rear of the body with a rolled pan to match the grille. Chrome exhaust stacks that ended at the leading edge of the frame rail wings were added to

A Personal Remembrance

In 1956, when I was 11, I lived three blocks from the gas station where "Chili" Catallo parked his three-window coupe while he worked at his family's nearby grocery store. It was the first real hot rod I had ever seen in person, and I was crazy about cars, especially hot rods. Every day after school, I'd ride up to that gas station and hope the car would be there. If it was, I'd hang around for an hour or more and drink in every detail of the car. I secretly hoped the owner would come over some day and say, "Hey kid, want to go for a ride?" Unfortunately, I was never asked, and I could only dream of what it would have been like riding in that coupe. Then one day the car was gone, and I was too shy to ask the guys in the gas station where it was.

That car left a big impression on me. Every model kit of a '32 coupe I built as a youngster had aspects of Catallo's coupe. Now that I'm building a real '32 five-window coupe, it will also reflect influences from Catallo's coupe. When I saw the coupe on the cover of *Hot Rod* magazine in 1961, the blue three-window had dramatically changed, but I knew it was the car I had fallen in love with a few years earlier. When I was contracted to do this book, I knew I had to find that car. With a little hard work and a little luck, I was able to contact the late owner's son, Curt, and was able to reconnect to this piece of my childhood. When I finally saw the car again in person, a chill ran up my spine.

When Catallo was driving the wheels off this coupe in the late 1950s, his travels included this trip to the drag strip. His three-window coupe would run the quarter in the 12-second range. On the engine is a McCulloch supercharger; the exhaust headers consist of unattractive flex tubing. This photo was taken prior to the addition of the Alexander Brother's custom nose. *Author's collection*

the engine. Hubcaps from a 1957 Plymouth were added with white plastic flippers. The interior and top insert were done in white Naugahyde with blue buttons. One of the Alexander Brothers' trademark touches was a pair of dual recessed antennas, added to the coupe's left rear quarter, where they also doubled as the switches for the electric door solenoids. In the late 1950s and early 1960s, cars were regularly given names, and Catallo's coupe was called the *Silver Sapphire*. This Michigan car was ahead of its time, and even a step ahead of California's hot rods.

The draw of the West Coast was too much for Catallo, and in 1960 he and the *Silver Sapphire* moved to California. He took a job at George Barris' shop and

Clarence "Chili" Catallo bought this coupe for $75 in 1956. He constantly changed and upgraded the coupe. In 1961 it was selected to be the cover car for *Hot Rod* magazine and subsequently ended up on the cover the Beach Boys *Little Deuce Coupe* record album. ©David Newhardt

Above: The unique nosepiece on Catallo's coupe was designed and built by the Alexander Brothers, Detroit's top 1960s era customizers. The grille's horizontal bars were handcrafted and floated on a mesh background. The rare Kinmont front brakes are chrome plated. ©David Newhardt

Left: Catallo changed many things over the lifetime of the coupe, but he remained faithful to the Olds engine. Its final version was topped with a 671 GMC supercharger, three Stromberg carburetors, and a lot of chrome plating. The gold Barris crest on the side of the cowl was added following the 3-inch top chop at George Barris' West Coast shop. ©David Newhardt

A large 1950s era Lincoln steering wheel dominates the interior of Catallo's coupe. The coupe's cramped interior was trimmed in pearl white and blue vinyl. ©David Newhardt

swept floors, while he attended college in Long Beach. It was at this point that the final major changes were made to the car. Barris chopped the top 3 inches. Junior Conway added a new shade of blue to the car, along with white scallops in a pattern similar to the silver ones. Chrome wheels replaced the Plymouth hubcaps, but the wide whitewalls remained in place. The final touch was the addition of a 671 GMC blower and three Stromberg carbs. It was a magnificent car. Catallo's coupe was trendy, but it still retained all of the traditional hot rod components.

In 1961, *Hot Rod* magazine editor Bob Greene sent Eric Rickman to photograph Catallo's coupe. The images from that photo shoot ended up on the cover and in a four-page spread within the magazine. Another famous '32 coupe, owned by Andy Kassa of Passaic, New Jersey, was also featured in that issue. When Capitol Records was ready to release another Beach Boys album, it needed a car that would be perfect for the cover and that was a true "little deuce coupe." Capitol contacted George Barris and he suggested Catallo's coupe. The shot that was used on the cover was one of Rickman's outtakes. Shortly after the album's release, Catallo sold his coupe. He was a constant tinkerer, and he had done everything possible he wanted to do with the car.

Catallo's coupe spent some time in a high school auto shop, but remained nearly intact for 30 years. The

Olds engine had been replaced with a Mopar wedge, and the original frame had been scrapped in favor of a reproduction set of rails. In 1996, with a little urging from his family, Catallo bought his car back, determined to restore it to its former glory. Unfortunately, two years into the project, Catallo died of a heart attack at the age of 58. His son Curt was determined to finish the project in honor of his father. With his dad's gigantic scrapbook in hand, Curt was able to restore the coupe. In 2000, Curt Catallo drove his father's coupe out onto the lawn at the Meadowbrook Concours d' Elegance. Fittingly, the hometown favorite won the People's Choice award. The coupe has gone on to be displayed at the Pebble Beach Concours and at the prestigious Petersen Automotive Museum in Los Angeles, California.

Gary Moline's Flathead Coupe

Gary Moline's '32 three-window was inspired by another chopped '32 coupe that appeared on the cover of *Hot Rod* magazine in 1957. The car was a deep

Gary Moline's chopped '32 three-window was heavily influenced by a deuce coupe he saw on the cover of a 1957 *Hot Rod* magazine. The body on Moline's coupe is a fiberglass reproduction manufactured by Downs. It's chopped and has exposed door hinges and a working cowl vent. Contrast was added to the car by adding purple paint on the frame, rear wheel houses, and firewall. The color came from his granddaughter's crayon box. The wheels are polished American mags mounted with BFG Radials.

A single chrome push-bar protects the rolled rear pan of Moline's three-window. The taillights are 1941 Chevy with blue dots.

maroon '32 three-window highboy with a 5-inch chop that was owned by Lloyd Bakan. It had bobbed fenders in the rear, motorcycle fenders in the front, and a Chrysler Hemi engine. Moline always liked the car's overall proportions, the heavily chopped roof, and its clean looks. The vision of that car bounced around in his head for almost 40 years before he took action.

Moline didn't want to create a clone of Bakan's coupe, but he wanted to take its best elements for his own hot rod. When he finally decided to act on his vision, he added a few more changes that made the car more to his liking. Moline started with a Downs fiberglass three-window coupe body. Like Bakan's original coupe, Moline selected his with a chopped top. He also specified a working cowl vent, rolled rear pan, exposed door hinges, and original-style exterior door handles. For a frame and suspension he went to Total Cost Involved (TCI) for one of its Stage III deuce chassis.

Moline looked to hot rod tradition for his coupe's flathead engine. He started with a late block and bored it 0.125 inch over to increase the displacement to 276 ci. Ross pistons, Chevy valves, and a Winfield

286-degree-duration camshaft are located inside. Two other Chevy components were modified to fit the early Ford engine: a distributor and a water pump. All Ford flathead engines came with a pair of small water pumps that mounted on the front of the block. Moline mounted a 409 Chevy water pump, which has extended legs, to the front of the engine. At first glance, Moline's flathead looks like any other conventional V-8 engine with a single pulley for the water pump, but Ford never made a single pump for its flathead engines. The addition of the center mount, a single pulley pump, allows the owner to have various accessory drive options that would be impossible with the flathead's standard dual pumps. Moline's engine is topped off with a pair of polished Offenhauser heads and an Offenhauser intake with a trio of Stromberg carbs.

An 11-inch clutch that's attached to a Ford top loader four-speed backs Moline's flathead. Ford top loaders are usually shifted by mechanical linkage with arms that attach to the side of the transmission. When a shifter is installed in a narrow body like a '32 coupe, it ends up too far back and too far to the left and requires a unique shifter lever. Moline adapted a Jeep shifter that bolts to the top of the transmission. This positioned the shifter in the center of the car and as far forward as the original '32 shifter. Moline's Jeep shifter gives him the vintage look with the durability of a modern transmission.

One of the first things you notice when you see Moline's coupe is the two-tone paint scheme. Ten years ago he saw a '34 coupe that was under construction. Its frame was painted, but the body was in primer. Moline liked the contrast and decided to paint

Left: The underside of Moline's three-window is as clean as the top. The center section on the rear axle is a polished Halibrand quick-change unit. Coil-over shocks and a rear sway bar improve handling. The custom stainless exhaust system is completely polished.

his coupe black, with the frame and fender wells painted a contrasting purple. Finding the right shade was a problem, but Moline's granddaughter assisted him with the color selection. A crayon pulled from her crayon box was the perfect shade he was looking for. In addition to the frame and fender wells, Moline also painted the firewall purple.

One of the toughest challenges Moline encountered was how to comfortably stuff his 6-foot, 4-inch frame into the small coupe. Even without a chopped top, a '32 coupe can be a little confining for anyone under 6 feet. Moline removed the package tray, moved the seat all the way back, and lowered the seat as much as possible. He then added 2 inches of head room by tossing out the bows that support the headliner, and gluing the headliner directly to the inside of the roof. The result is a roomy interior for someone over 6 feet.

Moline's coupe is so clean, it looks as if it must sit in a garage between car shows, but it's actually a daily driver with over 11,000 miles on the odometer. Moline confides that even without air conditioning, the factory-style cowl vent keeps the interior cool.

Mike Martin's Cammer Coupe

Mike Martin's yellow highboy is another three-window deuce coupe with a Ford engine, but it's not a flathead. Martin opted for the Ford single overhead cam 427, one of the baddest engines ever built. Martin teamed with Steve Davis, one of the best hot rod/race car builders on the West Coast, to build his deuce. Along the way he got a lot of his friends involved. "Everyone who helped me build this car is a friend," says Martin. "It was very important to me that only my friends be involved in the process of building a car. It's such a long-term commitment that I wanted to have fun with my friends." It's obvious that Martin has some talented friends!

Martin wanted to build a 1960s-style car only using components that were available in the 1960s.

The flathead engine on Moline's coupe has been built for speed, durability, and good looks. A 409 Chevy water pump replaced the original flathead's twin water pumps. The distributor is also a Chevy unit, and an alternator is used for electrical system charging. Plenty of chrome and polished aluminum nicely dress the engine.

The 1932 three-window has always been his favorite car, and the SOHC 427 was his choice because that's what powered Jack Chrisman's 1966 Funny Car. The first three-window body Martin bought turned out to be in such bad shape that it couldn't be salvaged. The second body was much more expensive, but was in great shape and perfect for Martin's project.

Martin had Pete Eastwood stretch and box the original frame rails. Many deuce builders stretch the frame to increase the wheelbase from 106 to 110 inches. This subtle change helps to reduce the stubbiness of the car.

The profile of Martin's three-window is classic hot rod. The wheelbase has been stretched from 106 to 110 inches. This increase helps reduce the stubbiness of the coupe body and allow for an extended engine compartment. The blend of these elements is evident in the perfect alignment of the exhaust collector to the frame rail.

The frame was also Ced front and rear so the car could sit lower. The front axle has a 4-inch drop and the rear has coil-overs with ladder bars. Martin regularly switches between three sets of wheels and tires: Halibrand "kidney beans," Halibrand five-spokes, and yellow painted steel wheels with hubcaps and trim rings. All of the wheels in Martin's collection are 15X4 inches wide for the front

tires, and 15X10 inches wide for the rear. All front wheels mount 145X15 Michelin tires and all rear tires are 265X15 Continental.

Those who know Steve Davis believe he was born with a hammer and dolly in one hand and a piece of sheet metal in the other. He learned his trade by working with top-notch builders like John Buttera. When

Martin is asked about the work Davis did on his coupe his answer is "extensive." Most of the changes are so subtle that the casual observer will never notice; the cowl was raised 3/4 inch, the corners of the doors and deck lid were slightly rounded, and the A-pillars were leaned back 1/2 inch. The more noticeable changes include the chopped top—1 3/8 inch in front and 1 inch in the rear. The roof was filled, and a rolled rear pan was added. The top of Davis' custom hood opens clamshell style. The sides of the hood have blisters added to create clearance for the SOHC engine's valve covers. Depending on his mood, Martin runs the car with or without the hood sides.

Art Chrisman built the SOHC 427 engine. Ford introduced the SOHC engine in 1965 to compete against the Chrysler Hemi. This unique engine featured a pair of chain-driven camshafts, one on each Hemi-style cylinder head. The SOHC engines were made only for racing, and none were ever installed on the production line. NASCAR quickly banned them, but

Blue leather covers the interior of Martin's '32 three-window. The instrument panel has a small custom fabricated switch panel added, along with a custom steering column drop. The package tray has been removed so the seat could be moved rearward to add more leg room.

Ford's SOHC was released in 1965 solely for racing. This engine powered all types of drag race cars from gassers to Top Fuel dragsters. The timing chain for the two cams is over 6 feet long. Dual Holley four-barrel carbs rest on a polished aluminum intake.

Beauty and function are combined in this Martin-fabricated combination headlight/shock mount. On most hot rods, these are two separate brackets that are built more for function than for form. Reversed spring eyes and a notched frame give the car a lower front stance.

NHRA and other drag racing sanctioning bodies allowed competitors to run them in Factory Experimental, Funny Car, and Top Fuel dragster classes. In addition to its excellent breathing ability, the overhead cam configuration allowed the engine to rev like a kitchen blender.

Martin's SOHC engine is equipped with a set of 9.5:1 forged pistons. The camshafts are stock Ford units, as is the crankshaft. Martin used a factory dual quad intake with twin Holley carbs, which was the same setup that was used on the Mustang A/FX racers. The ignition is a Vertex magneto. A custom set of stainless steel exhaust headers snake from the engine over the frame rails. When Martin turns the key, the big engine quickly rumbles to life. It has enough torque to gently rock the car from side to side when it idles, but it's docile enough to be driven in traffic. Behind the engine is a Ford C-6 transmission with a B&M 2,500-rpm stall converter. It's easy to hear the engine inside Martin's coupe because there's no radio or air conditioning. It's all hot rod deuce coupe.

Bob Berry's Hemi Coupe

Another three-window deuce coupe owner who likes big V-8s is Bob Berry. He started his deuce coupe project with only an engine. In 1995 Larry Holt of Speed Specialties built Berry a blown 392-ci Hemi engine. Berry has always had a fondness for Hemi engines. He installed a 331-ci Hemi in his first car, a 1957

Bob Berry's '32 three-window is based on a Wescott fiberglass body. Berry ordered the body from Wescott with exposed hinges, and he added a chrome windshield frame and exterior door handles to give it the look of an original steel body. The wheelbase was stretched 3 inches because of the length of the blown Hemi engine. The color is PPG Wild Orange.

Berry's coupe sits with a classic hot rod rake. The 15-inch diameter wire wheels mounted with big 'n' little radials have been painted silver. The taillights are '39 Ford teardrop with blue dots.

Plymouth Belvedere. In the 40 years since, most of Berry's cars have had Hemi engines, so it was no surprise to any of his friends when he had the Hemi powerplant built without having chosen a car. Once the engine was finished, he had to find a car in which to install it. "The '32 three-window coupe was a natural," quipped Berry with a smile.

Any Top Fuel driver would be proud of the engine Larry Holt built for Bob Berry. He started with a '57 Chrysler block and bored it slightly to displace 405 ci. To the stock rods, Holt added Aries 8:1 pistons. A Crower cam, lifters, and valve springs were installed next. Stainless steel valves were added to the stock Hemi heads. A polished BDS 671 blower serves two

Holley 600-cubic foot per minute carbs; a Vertex magne to bolted to the top of the engine provides the spark. Custom headers wrap outside the frame rails and connect to a pair of Ultra Flow mufflers. This combination is good enough to dyno 400 horsepower at the rear wheels.

Bob Berry selected a Wescott fiberglass chopped three-window deuce body and mounted it on a pair of Deuce Factory rails. Berry selected exposed hinges for the doors on his coupe, a chrome windshield frame, and stock door handles. These elements, along with the excellent proportions of the Wescott body, have fooled many into thinking it's a steel body. The car is painted Wild Orange. On the rear is a pair of '39 blue-dot taillights and a stock deuce gas tank.

The frame was stretched 3 inches to accommodate the big Hemi engine. Up front is a Magnum axle with a 5-inch drop attached to a chrome monospring. The 3.50 posi Ford 9-inch rear end is supported by Aldan coilovers. Wilwood discs provide the stopping power up front, while 11-inch drums bring up the rear. Silver paint and chrome trim rings accent the 15-inch diameter wire wheels that mount big 'n' little radials.

Henry Arroyo did the stitching for the simple black Naugahyde on the Glide bench seat and door panels. The dash is filled with Stewart Warner Wings gauges, and the four-spoke Bell steering wheel rests on a tilt column. Berry's interior has all the comforts of any luxury car, including a Vintage Air air conditioning system, stereo cassette player, and power windows. The Lokar shifter connects to the Turbo 400, which has been modified with a B&M shift kit.

Bruce Meyer's Ardun-Powered Coupe

Bruce Meyer's bright red three-window highboy coupe also runs a blown "Hemi" engine of sorts. The engine is a Ford flathead with an Ardun overhead conversion and an S.CO.T blower—a rare beast. Meyer started with a full-fendered steel-bodied three-window

The big Chrysler Hemi engine in Berry's coupe is vintage 1957. It displaces 405 ci and develops 400 horsepower at the rear wheels. The supercharger is a GMC 671 with two 600-cubic-foot-per-minute Holley carbs on top.

Above: Zora Arkus-Duntov, the father of the Corvette, designed the Ardun cylinder heads on Meyer's coupe. Their hemispherical combustion chambers were a great leap in technology in the days prior to the mass production of overhead valve engines. The only new component on the engine is the finned supercharger manifold, which was made to look as if were cast in the 1950s.

Left: Bruce Meyer had his '32 three-window built to early 1950s specs. He started with a car that had been chopped and made into a hot rod. Meyer was drawn to the car because of its Ardun-equipped flathead.

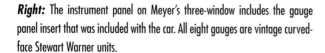

Above: The interior of Meyer's three-window is covered in black vinyl. The seat belts are aircraft-style, and the steering wheel is a 1940 Ford Deluxe. Chrome window frames accent the interior.

Right: The instrument panel on Meyer's three-window includes the gauge panel insert that was included with the car. All eight gauges are vintage curved-face Stewart Warner units.

Howard Gribble's chopped three-window highboy has a stealthy look. The former owner of Halibrand, a company that makes mag wheels and quick-change rear ends, owned this coupe at one time. It was outfitted with Halibrand's best, which included a set of 16-inch-diameter knock-off wheels.

that had been hot rodded in the 1950s and 1960s. One of the reasons he bought the coupe was because of the supercharged Ardun converted flathead that was in the car. The Ardun cylinder head conversion for the flathead was designed and first built over 50 years ago by Zora Arkus-Duntov, the father of the Corvette. Ardun

heads have a hemispherical combustion chamber that increases the engine's breathing ability and horsepower. Ardun heads were rare and expensive in the 1950s, and they're even more so today.

When Meyer got the car, the engine didn't run very well and the car's stance was all wrong. "Someone had just

The rear frame rails on Gribble's coupe have been bobbed, and a custom fuel tank has been placed inside the trunk. The rear spreader bar has a pair of built-in taillights, and a pair of '39 Ford teardrop lights are mounted horizontally on the rear of the body.

thrown Ardun heads on it and it didn't even run," says Meyer. "But when I saw the car, I knew it had the potential to be something that was real reminiscent of the 1950s." Dave Enmark of So-Cal Speed Shop reworked the engine. "When Enmark built the motor, I told him I didn't want a gun," recalls Meyer. "I want to put a lot of miles on this car, so build it as conservatively and as

strongly as you can." Enmark did his job well. Even with the blower, the engine starts easily and has a wide power band. The only newly manufactured part on the engine is the intake manifold, which was machined out of billet aluminum by Shane Wickerly of the So-Cal Speed Shop. The manifold has been carefully aged to look as if it were cast in the 1950s.

Above: From the size of the mail-slot windshield, it appears the front of the roof on Gribble's coupe has been chopped a little more than the rear. This is not an uncommon practice in the hot rodding world. The front brakes have Buick finned brake drums.

Right: Under the multilouvered hood of Gribble's three-window is a 350-ci small-block. Chevrolet ram's horn exhaust manifolds are used. These manifolds were used in the 1960s on Corvettes and passenger cars. Their simple design makes the installation of a small-block in deuce rails easy. Cast-iron manifolds are quieter and are not prone to cracking like tubular headers.

Other than the intake manifold, there isn't a part on Meyer's car that was manufactured after the 1950s. Even the unique gauge panel with its curved glass Stewart Warner gauges is the original one that was installed in the 1950s. "I have several roadsters, and I just thought it would be really cool to have a chopped highboy coupe," says Meyer. "It's never to late to have a happy childhood."

Howard Gribble's Halibrand Coupe

Howard Gribble's black three-window highboy also looks as if it had been built in the late 1950s. At one time, it was used in advertising for the Halibrand company. That's because the coupe was once owned by Barry Blackmore, a former owner of the Halibrand company. Fittingly, it is equipped with some of the most distinctive Halibrand components. The coupe's Halibrand quick-change rear end was among the best ever manufactured and it has a classic look that hot rodders love. Along with a quick-change rear end, Gribble's coupe runs authentic knock-off 16X5-inch "kidney bean" wheels on the front and 16X7s on the rear.

Gribble's coupe proves the point that a hot rod looks best when it's simple. He describes his no-frills approach to his deuce coupe as "a high-tech 1950s look." Without question, the louvered hood, filled grille shell, and classic hot rod Buick finned aluminum front brake drums exemplified the 1950s look. The interior is a pleated red Naugahyde with a Bell sprint car-style four-spoke steering wheel, and it has Simpson racing seat belts. Under the hood is a stock small-block Chevy. It can't get much simpler than that.

The milled stainless upper and lower control arms of the Kugel-built independent front suspension are visible under the fenders of Bill Lewis' three-window coupe. Lewis puts a lot of miles on each year, and he wanted an improved ride and handling.

The engine in Lewis' coupe is a 1995 Corvette LT4. With the exception of the exhaust headers and a little custom paint, the engine is completely stock. The accessory on the near side of the engine is the compressor for the air conditioning system. An electric fan is attached to the rear of the aluminum radiator, and the firewall is custom, with a recess for the engine.

Bill Lewis' Full-Fendered Coupe

At the opposite end of the deuce three-window spectrum is the coupe owned by Bill Lewis. He took a different approach when he built his all-steel, full-fendered three-window. Like most of the deuces in this book, it was built to be a daily driver. Since 1983 it has made five trips to the East Coast from California for hot rod events,

and it is a fixture at all West Coast rodding events. Between 1993 and 1995, Lewis completely rebuilt his coupe and made something good into something great.

Lewis added an SAC frame and Kugel polished stainless independent front suspension. The independent rear suspension is based on a Corvette unit and features Kugel's custom components. The front and rear disc

Late-model bucket seats were added to Lewis' coupe for driving comfort. An overhead console houses the CD changer controls. A leather-wrapped banjo steering wheel is mounted on a tilt column.

brakes are power assisted. The steering is a Kugel rack and pinion. Lewis' coupe has a suspension with no equal. The engine Lewis selected is a 1995 Corvette LT4 with electronic fuel injection. It's backed by a 700R4 transmission. The fuel injection and overdrive transmission provide a flexible combination that's both powerful and stingy on fuel.

Because Lewis puts on a lot of miles each year, he wanted to have the interior as comfortable as possible. Late model bucket seats are covered in a combination of leather and tweed. A wool carpet covers the floor. An overhead console controls the Panasonic sound system that includes a CD changer. A tilt column and air conditioning have also been installed.

Ford's '32 three-window coupe is a classic design, and hot rodders have taken advantage of its good looks and made it look even better. The distinctive suicide doors made the three-window a standout in Ford's 1932 line-up of cars. The three-window's timeless lines look great with or without fenders, and with or without a chopped top. The 1932 Ford, in any body style, will always be the icon for the American hot rod.

The personalized license plate declares Lewis' pride that his coupe is all steel. The taillight is a stock '32 unit with a built-in license plate light.

Retro Rods

Dan Burger and Robert Genat

I can think of at least two ways that the construction of a book is similar to building a retro rod: The parts come from a hundred different places, and the help of others can get you through some things that you would never figure out on your own.

I'd like to thank several southern California car clubs: the Deacons, Shifters, Choppers, Auto Butchers, and Lucky Ducks. The members of these clubs are building and driving some incredible rods and customs.

I talked to a lot of club members about their cars and the definition and parameters of retro-rodding and then combined it in the best way I could to make this book insightful for those unfamiliar with this corner of the automotive hobby. Those who were particularly helpful include Jonny Guilmet, Morgwn Penneypacker, John Bade, Mick Rossler, Alex "Axle" Idzardi, Johnny "The Ghoul" Greybeck, Mike Ibbetson, Jon "Fish" Fisher, Jeff Vodden, and Tom Branch.

From the "older" generation of hot-rodders, I'd like to thank Joe Reath, John Guilmet, Tom Leanardo, Jim Richardson, and Reid Carroll for their insights, recollections, and observations.

Others who took time to assist me include Rob Fortier, John Logghe, Howard Gribble, Charlie Thorpe, Alan Averhoff, Vince Yamasaki, Ali, Colleen, Paul Rebmann, Chuck Edwald, Don Garlits, Zack Norman, Bill Franey, Aaron Kahan, Sam Davis, Ken Gross, Dennis Mitosinka, and Clyde and Gail Bangiola.

I think a car book without pictures would be worse than a world without hot rods. Well, maybe not that bad, but trust me, neither you nor I would like it. So a big thanks to Robert Genat whose hard work developed into fantastic photos that made this book a true chronicle of retro rod creations.

—Dan Burger

INTRODUCTION

This Looks Vaguely Familiar

If the second time around is better than the first, then what is the third? Hot-rodding offered a second life for many haggard, beaten, thrashed, and trashed automobiles. These cars had been put out to pasture and left unprotected from the ravages of time and the punishments of rain, snow, sun, and wind. Machines that were created for the road, had a purpose, and provided service no longer turned a crank or blinked a light. Rather than allowing these vehicles to sink up to their axles in mud and the engines turn to stone, young men with wild ideas and a few dollars in their pockets rescued them and took them home.

In the course of building their dream machines, these young men made the old cars look young again. They took the feeble and enabled them to run faster than ever. I'm not going to say they healed the sick and raised the dead. That would take a miracle. Hot-rodders aren't miracle workers, but they are definitely hard workers. I've seen their garages. If you listen to the original hot-rodders tell stories for a while, it's a miracle some of them are still alive.

Hot rods have been around for as long as there have been automobiles, but the term only gained widespread use in the years after World War II. Hot-rodding picked up momentum in the early 1950s and then took off like an accelerator pedal stuck to the floorboard. Its popularity was a phenomenon not unlike the rock and roll music popular at that same time. There were people who strongly believed Satan had a hand in both; however, my research discovered no evidence that this was, in fact, the case.

The most striking similarity between hot-rodding and rock and roll was that they each were emblematic of a break from the mainstream. They were anything and everything but ordinary and underscored a desire by those involved to think differently and be different.

That's just one aspect of hot-rodding, however. There was more than one reason for its popularity.

Building a rod or a custom is like putting together a puzzle with some of the pieces missing. It provides not only the challenge of the puzzle but the opportunity to make the puzzle fit the individual rather than the other way around. As a builder you are bound by hard-and-fast mechanical principles on

This channeled Model A roadster was built and driven by Ron and Gene Logghe. The Logghe brothers later gained national recognition for building drag racing chassis. *John Logghe Collection*

one hand, and you are completely free to set new creative boundaries on the other. There is great satisfaction to be found in projects that involve both discipline and creativity. It allows individuality to show, and that's why these cars are some of the greatest automobiles of all time. People poured so much time and effort into them. The hot rod ethic was completely different than the mass-consumption, standardization of cars. It's ironic that Henry Ford built an empire on that standardized principle, and the rod and custom builders used the same products to create entirely different cars.

The process of building a rod or custom during this era also had the appeal of a treasure hunt. There was little opportunity for off-the-shelf buying. Instead of "I want it, I'll buy it," it was "I want it, I'll build it." Maybe it was the pioneering spirit or self-reliance that came with taking the road less traveled.

The retro-rodders of today exhibit many of those same traits. They appreciate what it took to build a rod or custom in 1955 and recognize the individuality of those cars. It was a highly creative time, and many of those cars vanished from the scene. It's good to see the retro-rodders preserving what they can to build old-school rods and customs that honor the originals. This makes it the third time around for some of those old jalopies. They make sense of funny sayings such as, "It's déjà vu all over again."

This Olds-powered rod was built in Detroit in the mid- to late-1950s. The challenge of building a retro style hotrod is gaining popularity 50 years after originals like this one prowled the streets and strips. *John Logghe Collection*

CHAPTER ONE

When does a rod become retro? The term *retro rod* could easily be considered redundant. After all, aren't all rods retro? That question can be answered "a little bit, yes, but a little bit more, no." It takes a good eye and some familiarity with hot rod history to make distinctions. Even with those skills, the boundaries of retro are open to different interpretations.

Hot-rodding covers a lot of ground. It has always been an experimental speed laboratory most often operating out of the corner of some back alley garage. It began with the dawn of automobile creation. As soon as someone had a car, there was someone else who wanted a car that was faster. Look in the automotive history books. There were always gearheads who wanted to strip down a car body to the bare necessities and build up an engine until it breathed fire, roared like a monster, and set new records for scorched earth.

Although the basic tenets of hot-rodding were in place, the one-of-a-kind, built-for-speed, do-it-yourself customs weren't called hot rods until the wild automotive experience that exploded just after World War II. This particular era—from 1946 until the early 1960s—was the crucible of hot-rodding as we know it today. The cars that were stripped down, the engines that were built up, and the collaborative efforts that went into these one-of-a-kind, home-built, street-and-track racers are milestones in the rich

Take a Model A Ford roadster, drop in some vintage 1960s power—such as a small-block Chevy that was separated from its Corvette body—and you've got a good start toward a retro rod that will win praise and admiration.

Halibrand knock-off wheels are a rare accessory item from the 1950s era. Hairpin radius rods are a classic addition. The owner of this Model A hot rod built his own when he could not a pair one that had the right look for his rod.

American automotive heritage. The cars, technology of that era, enthusiasm for automotive adventures, and the place in this country's history combined to make these hot rods some of the greatest cars to roll down blacktop anywhere.

Exact definitions for hot rods are seldom agreed upon, but the parameters for a modern-day retro rod generally coincide with the hot rods that were created during the time frame mentioned above. The choices for body, frame, engine, and accessories were truly whatever was handy, but certain styles prevailed and certain engines excelled. A combination of supply and demand, trial and error, and throwing caution to the wind produced incredible ingenuity.

The popularity and notoriety of hot-rodding shifted into high gear as America became car crazy in the late 1940s and early 1950s. Because new car production was shut down during World War II, between 1942 and 1945, demand was miles ahead of supply. Even though early postwar production consisted of warmed-over prewar models, the clamor for new cars was like a tide moving in and sweeping the dealers' showrooms clean. With each year after the war, new car production picked up. The used car business was also brisk as many older cars were traded in. These used vehicles, plus the abundance of junkyard iron from the 1920s and 1930s, became the fuel for the hot rod fires.

As America traveled through the 1950s, new car development created a horsepower race that placed an emphasis on power and speed. This was especially true in the low-priced cars where economy had always taken precedence over speed. The mass-market cars developed tremendous brand loyalty, and pride of ownership became increasingly dependent on performance attributes. In addition to that, a growing popularity for auto racing also rubbed off on young people looking for excitement.

Another big reason for the increasingly widespread appeal of hot-rodding during this time was the introduction of the rodding enthusiast publications. The biggest and most well known was *Hot Rod*, a Los Angeles–based monthly magazine produced by Petersen Publications. Along with the standard-sized *Hot Rod* were the

The Model A retro rod interior is simple and to the point. Six gauges provide all the necessary information, interior panels are made of wood, and the small underdash heater box has been chromed. A Mexican blanket across the seats is a favorite southern California accessory.

miniature format magazines such as *Rod & Custom*, *Honk!* (later *Car Craft*), and *Hop Up*. These magazines were filled with photos of the coolest rods and customs along with how-to advice for the growing legion of hot-rodding enthusiasts.

The Hollywood factor was thrown in as hot rod movies became a sure way to attract a teenage crowd to the drive-in theaters. Although the depiction was far from accurate, the big screen put hot-rodding in the spotlight along with rock and roll music.

Find it. Buy it. Build it.

The basic hot rod formula consisted of a cheap, bare bones body and a high-

Attention to detail can go to great lengths. This chopped roadster is a 1950s-style hot rod showpiece. Take note of the beautiful folding top, the drilled front axle, and the 16-inch wheels.

performance engine. It doesn't sound like much, but it prompted creativity to blossom as hot-rodders took a completely different road than the one the major auto makers were on. Factory assembly lines were stamping out bigger, heavier, more luxury-laden and expensive mass-produced cars, and they were selling like hot dogs on the Fourth of July. The hot rods were smaller and more Spartan, but noticeably quicker and more exciting. They were also built to individual desires and funded by part-time or first-job-out-of-school paychecks. Those who could skillfully handle a wrench and a cutting torch took the place of automotive designers and production workers and built the car young America could relate to.

Just about everyone living in 1950s America said Detroit was building the American dream and the hot-rodders were creating an American nightmare. Hot rods were outside the boundaries of mainstream American thinking, and the guys who built and drove them were seen as renegades. That reputation was all the better for those who wanted to break

away from the herd. The attainment of nonconformist status played a huge role in the enduring interest in hot rods and hot-rodders. A cool set of wheels was the signature statement for those who chose to think differently.

Most hard core hot-rodders probably wouldn't disagree with the nonconformist description, especially if conforming meant having to settle for the assembly-line cars made for the average American family. But thinking outside the box is not, in and of itself, enough to make a worthy hot rod. Hot-rodders were more than renegades. They were also planners, engineers, designers, and test pilots. Within their network of friends, they put together impromptu automotive research and development departments. They ventured out to the cutting edge, pushing development but maintaining self-imposed fiscal restraint. In many cases the most important role may have been the treasure hunter. Hot-rodders picked over the boneyards where abandoned and abused junk lay rusting away. Parked in farmers' fields, an old shed, or sometimes the back row on the used car lot were the bargain purchases that make great stories

A Ford banjo-style steering wheel and Auburn dash add class and clearly differentiate this car from the modern street rods that use billet as brightwork.

even when they aren't mixed with beer and fabrications of the truth.

For a lot of car enthusiasts, the hunt is the best part of getting a car back on the road. It's like being a detective. There are investigations, you chase down leads that are often dead ends, and you find what you want, but you may not be able to pry it loose.

One rodder's story recounts an attempt to buy a 1932 five-window coupe. The opportunity took place 17 years ago when he was in high school. The owner of the car wanted $2,000 for it, and the high school kid tried to imagine where he'd come up with that kind of money. He knew one thing though: He had to have that car. It had the potential to be just like the John Milner car in *American Graffiti*. During the negotiation process the owner decided he didn't want to sell the car. It was an opportunity lost, and these kinds of opportunities don't come around often.

In this case, however, opportunity returned for a second visit. Seventeen years later the rodder returned to see if

Channeling the body over the frame rails was a nice touch that creates a distinctive look, especially noticeable around the rear tires. This red-primered 1932 three-window coupe is also chopped.

Stripped-down cars with built-up engines were usually built on a budget with more money going into the engine and suspension equipment than the cosmetics. This Model A roadster features cool headers, hairpin radius rods, finned Buick brake drums, Buick Nailhead engine, ´32 Ford grille shell, and a Duvall-style windshield.

by chance the car was still around. It was and so was the owner. The rodder says, "I tried to buy this car from you 17 years ago when I was in high school and you wouldn't sell it to me. What do you want for it now?"

"What did I tell you when you were in school?" the owner said.

"$2,000."

"Then it's $2,000 still."

The opportunity to buy that coupe did not pass by the rodder again. He gladly took the deal. "That car was my life's destiny," he told me. "There's no other car I ever wanted."

Salvage Yard Speculations

Most rods of this era began with vehicle bodies dating back to the 1920s, with the majority being factory-built

In-progress street rods are in the majority at retro rod events. Cars like these are driven sometimes daily in areas where the weather permits.

passenger cars from the 1930s. To a lesser extent, certain 1940s- and 1950s-era vehicles are also included in the retro rod family. Getting something cheap was the primary reason for latching on to something that was 15 to 25 years old or older. Hot rod project cars always had more cash (although generally not much more) designated for engines and mechanical components than they did for cosmetic touches. The majority of 1950s-era hot-rodders were rebuilding used engines that ranged from the early 1930s to several years behind the current models. The latest technology and the most modern engines and mechanicals

RIGHT
The radiator guard on this Deuce coupe is a great retro accessory item. Devil artwork is popular with the retro-rodders because it symbolizes a nonconformist attitude.

Open hoods with fully exposed engines are the most common look for the retro-rodders. In this case, a 1960s-era Pontiac tri-power engine is on display.

The bright blue paint and chrome wheels on this five-window coupe give it a late 1950s or early 1960s appearance. Retro-rodders generally believe the early 1960s were the final days of vintage hot-rodding.

made it into only the bigger-budget rods that were comparatively rare.

The remains of Chevys, Plymouths, and Fords have always been particularly easy to find. These cars were produced as basic commodities like bottles of ketchup or pairs of shoes. Long production runs on these mass-produced vehicles made parts interchangeability a better bet when buying a thoroughly worn-out vehicle. If the chosen junker didn't come completely equipped, spare parts could be located easily, or creative adaptations could be fabricated. Knowing what combination of parts worked best was one thing, knowing where to find them was another. In a way it was like mining for gold.

Out in the salvage yard ocean of potential hot rods, the Fords stood out. This was partly due to the sheer number of cars Ford Motor Company let loose on the streets. Model T and Model A Fords once covered the highways like ants on their way to a broken bag of sugar. What truly separated the Fords from the Chevys and Plymouths, which were also cheap and plentiful, was the connection Ford had with aftermarket speed equipment manufacturers. This bountiful relationship began in the days when Ford built only four-cylinder engines. The speed junkies of that era drove cars with stripped-down bodies known as speedsters. Modified Model T and Model A Ford engines were the most popular setup for street and track during the 1920s and 1930s. Chevy and Dodge-powered speedsters were much less common, and performance parts were almost nonexistent.

The Fords were not only an affordable product, they could be upgraded readily to produce a much higher level of performance. The Ford Motor Company benefited from this performance opportunity through the Model T and Model A era. When Ford introduced the V-8 in 1932, the high-performance speed

The flathead Fords ruled hot-rodding for many years, but with the introduction of the overhead-valve V-8 by Cadillac in 1949, a change was underway. This Model A roadster is packing an early Cadillac OHV V-8.

equipment manufacturers that had been with them for years followed along.

It's a common misconception that the Ford V-8 immediately claimed the high-performance throne, but in reality the hopped-up four-cylinder engines held their own for seven or eight years until the latter part of the 1930s. Take into consideration that a four-cylinder Ford with one of the aftermarket overhead-valve conversion kits could pump out 100 horsepower, and a factory stock V-8 was rated at 65 horsepower. As the overall economy climbed from the worst of the Depression years and sales of the V-8 Ford continued to rise, more speed equipment was produced and the flathead's popularity as a "poor man's" performance engine skyrocketed.

By the late 1940s and early 1950s, there were millions of Ford V-8s in existence. This resulted in an ample supply of used engines at prices that were easy on the pocketbook. The timing was right for young guys looking to build their own creations and get a lot of bang for the buck.

Although hot-rodding was basically an anything goes endeavor, one vehicle rises above all others when it comes to hot rods: the 1932 Ford, reverently referred to as The Deuce. It has ruled over postwar hot-rodding without ever losing the right stuff. This one-year-only body style is so popular that reproductions, in both steel and

fiberglass, have been produced and sold well for many years. Unfortunately there have never been enough of Deuce body originals to satisfy the hot-rodders' lust.

Deuce roadsters are the most prized body style. Hot-rodders during the 1950s quickly snatched these up because they were lightweight and cheap. In most cases the fenders and bumpers were thrown away because the rodders were looking to reduce weight. If anyone had thought about how expensive those fenders and bumpers would be today, no one would have thrown them away.

Because the design of the 1932 Fords placed the body on top of the frame rails, the rods that retained the stock configuration were known as "highboys." The unique 1932 frame rails make the car a highboy. The term also applies to Model T and Model A bodies that were set on Deuce rails. These bodies were even lighter than the equivalent Deuce roadster, coupe, or sedan, so it became a common hot-rodding practice to take advantage of even greater weight savings of the Model A and Model T Fords. The highboy is a hot-rodding icon, but the 1932 Ford rod comes in many great flavors.

When Flatheads Roamed the Earth

When it comes to retro-style hot-rodding, the Ford flathead V-8s (1932–1953) are the overwhelming choice

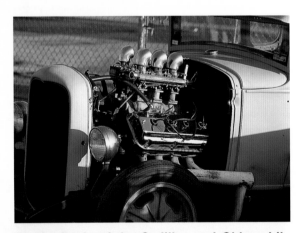

On the heels of the Cadillac and Oldsmobile overhead-valve engines was the Chrysler OHV hemi head engine. At the drags and out on the dry lakes, the big hemis kicked butt. When a hemi showed up in a street rod, it turned heads. This hemi is topped with a log-style manifold and six Stromberg carburetors.

Fenderless cars dominate the retro-rodders, but bobbed rear fenders were not uncommon on the original rods. This rod was originally built in the late 1950s. After being driven for several years it was put away and forgotten until it was recently discovered. It still wears its original lime green paint.

for the right look, sound, and feel. In their day, flathead V-8s ruled. Not only were they inexpensive and convenient to find, they were an easy fit into almost any body a hot-rodder had on hand. This was especially true for the numerous Model T and Model A bodies that were available. A hot-rodder was actually making it easy on himself by hopping up the V-8 and dropping it into a T or an A. The V-8 engine wasn't any longer than a four cylinder, so the swap was fairly easy. The V-8 transmission also fit neatly into the older, cheaper models. It was a script that played

The round 1950 Pontiac taillights were often chosen for 1950s-era rods. The license plate lights are another indicator of age. There are not many original rods in this, or any other condition, around.

out again and again for rodders from coast to coast. Mercury engines, a nearly identical cousin to the Ford flathead, were a treasured upgrade commonly seen in the original hot rods as well.

When the Ford V-8 was introduced in 1932, the performance-tuned Ford four-cylinder cars produced more horsepower than the stock V-8. The reason behind this was the number of aftermarket performance parts manufacturers that built equipment for Ford and other four-cylinder cars. Performance parts for the four-cylinder Model A engines were ready around the same time the cars rolled off the assembly line. Hot-rodding still had quite a few stalwarts who believed in the original Ford four-bangers and enjoyed

making a four run faster than most of the new sixes and eights, but driving a V-8 had great allure. Off the showroom floor, the new 221-cubic inch Ford flathead was cranking out 65 horsepower. These engines had 5.5:1 compression and were equipped with a single-barrel carburetor made by Detroit Lubricator. One year later horsepower was increased to 75, and a year after that it jumped to 85.

The Ford flathead remained a 221-cubic-inch displacement from 1932 through 1942, but in late 1938 the famous 21-stud cylinder head was converted to a 24-stud design that would carry through the remainder of its production years. In 1937 Ford introduced the 136-cubic-inch V-8 60—an economy V-8, rated at 60 horsepower, that was produced for four years.

With the introduction of the Mercury automobile in 1939 came a 239-cubic-inch Mercury flathead engine that was rated at 95 horsepower, 10 horsepower more than the Ford. For the short production run in 1942, it was increased to 100 horsepower. After the war, Ford and Mercury shared this

RIGHT
The suicide front axle setup on this sweet little roadster is a cool alternative to the standard dropped axles. This is another original early 1950s hot rod that stayed on the street long enough to go through several updates until it was purchased by retro-rodder Tom Branch who was interested in returning it to its original condition. Fortunately photos exist that will assist his efforts.

A chopped top and big ´n´ little tires give this 1932 Ford three-window coupe the profile that rodders of every vintage have fallen in love with. Four rows of louvers and the Halibrand racing wheels make the rod a personal statement.

100-horsepower engine until Mercury introduced a stroked, 255-cubic-inch, 110-horsepower version in 1949. Mercury stayed with the 255-cubic-inch engine until flathead engine production ceased with the debut of the 1954 lineup; however, in 1952 and 1953 the engine was rated at 125 horsepower. Meanwhile the last two years of 239-cubic-inch Ford flatheads were rated at 110.

Flathead fanatics generally agree that the Ford cylinder blocks could be safely bored to 3.375 (3 3/8) without creating an overheating problem due to thin cylinder walls. The prewar Ford flatheads had a factory bore of 3.062, and the postwar Fords were bored to 3.187. Rebuilding a flathead to get the most out of it involved porting, relieving, balancing, and blueprinting. Racing cams, intake manifolds supporting as many as six single-barrel carbs, and performance ignitions were all key ingredients. With high-performance heads the stock 5.5:1 compression ratio could be pushed to 9.5:1. Realistic expectations for these performance-built engines were in the neighborhood of 250 horsepower. More than 12 million Ford flatheads were built during its 22-year run.

The simple red paint used on the wire wheels and grille is an excellent complement to the primer black body and is perfect for a retro rod.

Joe Reath of Long Beach, California, was particularly adept at wringing power out of the flatties. Reath had a reputation on the streets and the strip. Reath Automotive is still a recognized name for many flathead owners who buy parts or have engines built there. As good as Reath

is with the flatheads, he's every bit as good at telling tales of hot-rodding's glory days.

Reath remembers buying a 1940 Ford coupe after starting his first job after high school. "I bought it from a guy called The Smiling Irishman who had a car lot on Figueroa Avenue in Los Angeles. The car had 18,000 miles on it, and I gave him $950. The first thing I did was put a set of Smitty's mufflers on it. Everybody had to have a pair of Smitty's. Then I went down to Eastern Auto Supply (later Cal Custom Supply) and bought a pair of fender skirts. On the way home, crossing over a railroad track, one of the skirts flew off and a semi truck ran over it. I'll never forget that."

When Reath started in on the motor, he first bored it out and "played with it a little bit." Then he went to Eddie Meyer's shop and bought a set of heads and a manifold. Those were the early days of what would become a lifetime of adventures on the streets, dry lakes, and drag strips for Reath.

There were, of course, many exceptions to flathead power. Chevy loyalists had high-performance heads and multicarb manifolds available for their inline sixes, and the GMC engine, which was slightly larger and stronger, was not uncommon. Dodge and Studebaker enthusiasts were also among the hot rod ranks. It was a wide-open field with an anything goes just-run-what-ya-brung attitude. The six-cylinder engines developed high torque as a result of long strokes and large pistons, and rodders could take advantage of this by using higher gear ratios. Most sixes could take considerable reboring without nearly the concern for thin walls that was inherent with V-8s. Reboring brings greater cubic inch displacement and with it more horsepower.

Although the aftermarket performance parts industry was heavily weighted toward Ford, there was an expanded effort beyond Ford in the early postwar years. Obviously the manufacturers had come to the conclusion that some rodders would rather drink gasoline than pour it into a Ford, and there was business in some of the other camps.

The 1949 introduction of the modern overhead-valve (OHV) V-8 engines by Cadillac and Oldsmobile set the stage for a new era in hot-rodding. It would take some time to gain acceptance and for old habits to die, but change was on the way. The overhead valve was a smooth-running engine design that immediately raised the performance bar. The extra power and performance, however, came with a higher price tag and a few more pounds to lug around. Two years after the Cad/Olds OHV breakthrough, Chrysler added an overhead-valve V-8 to its engine selection. It established a performance image with its hemi head design. By the time Pontiac and Buick joined the OHV V-8 parade, Ford had the

The retro look favors bias-ply tires in either wide whitewalls or blackwalls with the big 'n' little combination preferred. Steel wheels with baby Moon hubcaps are most common, but spinner-style hubcaps, Moon discs, and old-fashioned wire wheels are also popular.

flathead ready for retirement and began offering an OHV V-8 of its own.

Traditions die slowly. It took several years before the OHV Cadillacs, Oldsmobiles, and Chryslers began to take hold. Even then they weren't commonly seen in hot rods that were built strictly for street use. Those Cadillacs, Oldsmobiles, and Chryslers that did show up in rods got a lot of attention though. The same is true today in the retro rods. A rod with a 331-cubic-inch Cadillac, a Dodge Red Ram, or an Olds Rocket 98 will really draw a crowd.

Full-fendered and without a chopped top, this original ´32 Ford coupe is unique. It was built between 1956 and 1958 and still wears the paint and interior of that time.

A common dilemma for rod builders then and now is whether the engine will fit into the body and frame that awaits it. The hot rod magazines of the period are filled with questions about how to make specific engine, drivetrain, body, and frame combinations work. Issues regarding length, width, height, and weight make some combinations a winning or losing battle. Bigger, heavier engines affect a lot of other components from steering to springs to overpowering the rear end.

Regardless of the technical difficulties, hot-rodding advanced with the times.

Without a doubt the tide was turning, and when Chevrolet introduced its first V-8 in 1955, a monumental shift was about to take place. Chevy's overhead-valve V-8 was both powerful and lightweight. Performance enhancements came on the heels of its debut, and it became a hot rod favorite. Beginning with a 265-cubic inch displacement in two years it grew to 283 cubic inches, and five years later, 327 cubic inches.

Because hot-rodding was inexorably tied to guys with flat rather than fat wallets, cars were usually built with whatever was on hand. Anything that was cheap or free usually had priority status. If that meant building up an inline six, then that's the way it went. If there was a choice, most rodders went with a Ford roadster or coupe powered by a Ford flathead. Ford dominated the scene because it had the low-buck performance edge. First of all, there are two more cylinders than Chevy or a Plymouth, and second, the choices for performance upgrades were far better.

As the modern V-8s became more popular in the mid- to late 1950s, hot-rodding was in transition. Adding to the changing scenery were the postwar used cars that were being chopped, channeled, and lowered along with the traditional prewar hot rod favorites. Late 1940s and early 1950s Fords, Mercurys, and Chevys were out front. High-performance engines remained a primary ingredient, and many of these late-model hot rods were worthy street and track competitors, but many were being modified so radically that they were more of a design statement than a performance tour de force. The customs were displaying a new type of creativity and showmanship born right out of the postwar hot rod scene. It was a way to make an individual automotive statement and to be a gearhead.

In typical late 1950s style, this rod was originally equipped with an Olds J2 engine, and the front suspension is state-of-the-art 1956 Chevy, an uncommon choice.

On the Retro Road

The hot-rodders' turf is more varied than any other automotive realm. It's legitimate to say a hot rod is just about anything you want it to be. Distinctions between one type of rod and another are identifiable basically by applications of automotive technology available at any given time. Although modern street rods have a lot in common with the original rods, they are also removed from the original rods by 50 years of technology. Modern street rods take full advantage of the latest advances in automotive science that contributes to more powerful engines, better handling suspensions, more comfort, and convenience. A modern street rod is the natural evolution of a hot rod. Even this description is, at best, a generalization. As has always been the case, some rods are built to go, some are built to show, and many are somewhere on the road between those two points.

The retro rod, however, is a different animal. For the retro-rodder there was an era when the hot rod was perfect. It was pure and raw. Hot-rodding was a special turf where players needed to know the game in order to get in. Retro rods celebrate that era, ingenuity, and the cars that were created. The rods and customs of that era represent devotion and an enthusiasm that was the epitome of what many enthusiasts believe the hobby should be.

Because of the combination of mostly rosy economic and social circumstances in the years

The retro rod style allows latitude for many variations. This 1934 Ford five-window coupe has the quarter windows filled in for a unique look. The car is owned by Alex "Axle" Idzardi, president of the Shifters in Orange County, California.

Oldsmobile's Rocket V-8s were hot throughout the 1950s. They built a solid reputation with the rodders because the engines delivered a ton of torque.

following World War II, hot rods will be forever associated with that technological timeframe. Jobs were plentiful, and America's manufacturing engine was hitting on all its cylinders. Any young buck with an idea, a cheap car, and a little bit of cash could have a hell of a lot of fun building his own rod or custom with his buddies. Before that slice of American pie disappears almost unnoticed, the retro-rodders are pulling it out of history's ditch and putting it on the road again.

Take a closer look at what the retro rods are all about. First of all they are very personal statements. Instead of factories building cars for the masses, these are individual creations. The original hot rods,

and now the retro rods, are what car lovers do when left to their own devices. Most were built with dreams of speed and side-by-side racing, but they also needed to serve as daily drivers. Few factory cars could ever match them when it comes to bold individuality and an uninhibited, unconditional, freewheeling desire for performance and style. For that reason, hot rods rank right up there with the greatest cars ever built in this country.

Recreating the Perfect Rod

To build a retro rod you need to know about the originals. What was used to build them back then is what is used to build them now. Most retro-rodders pick an era, such as the early 1960s, and use few, if any, parts that are more modern than that era. Of course, most of the parts, including the body and frame, were 20, 30, and 40 years old at the time the rod was built in the 1960s.

Hot rods take shape as you build them. That's the opinion of Johnny Greybeck, a member of the Lucky Devils Car Club in Orange County, California. Club members and other friends in the hot rod ranks call him by his nickname "The Ghoul."

The Ghoul and most of the other Lucky Devils drive retro-style hot rods they more or less built themselves. For the most part, the rods are true to the 1950s and 1960s era of hot-rodding. Greybeck's rod is a fenderless 1931 Ford coupe painted with black primer. The 327-cubic-inch Corvette engine is fully exposed. Three Rochester carbs on a Weiand intake manifold stand out at first glance. A closer look reveals homemade headers that Greybeck salvaged from a bucket T that he once owned. He likes them because they have that butchered look that was often seen on personally built hot rods of the 1950s. This machine is both a retro rod and a daily driver. It was built to stand out from the modern street rods and to handle the rigors of day-to-day driving. He chose the 327 Chevy engine because it's more reliable than a flathead Ford. The engine

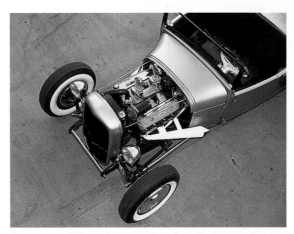

Anyone with an interest in classic hot rods can appreciate the attention to detail exhibited in this Model A roadster. This is what hours in the garage will produce.

This chopped Model A Ford coupe is a good example of the type of car that attracts the younger retro-rodders. A lot of people between the ages of 25 and 35 are getting involved in building and driving retro rods. This car is owned by Johnny Greybeck, a member of the Lucky Devils.

was bored .060 and makes use of a high-performance cam and roller rockers.

Following the parameters of building rods like they used to, Greybeck put his rod together with genuine 1950s and 1960s hot rod parts and accessories, some of which would have come from bone yard donor cars dating back to the 1930s and 1940s. The front brakes and wishbones are from a 1940 Ford. The shock mounts are cut and altered from a Ford F-1 pickup. The headlight brackets are modified 1932 Ford, as is the front spring, radiator, and shell. A 1936 Ford front spring is used on the rear of this car.

Greybeck fabricated the instrument panel faceplates in an original style. He also made use of a 1956 Chevy ignition switch, a 1949 Montgomery Wards heater, a vintage Klaxon horn, and a steering wheel from a 1940 Ford. The steering wheel includes a customized insert in the center, plus a 1950s-style steering-wheel knob. The BLC aftermarket headlights are a perfect vintage accessory, as are the dropped axle and the Moon fuel block. The coupe body for his rod is from an original car, as opposed to a reproduction body. Reproduction fiberglass bodies are available from several manufacturers. On the Ghoul's car the top was chopped 3 inches. The visor is louvered to give it a definite 1950s hot rod attitude.

The uniqueness of the original hot rods and the lack of documentation on how to build any one rod correctly leaves a lot to the whims of the owner. Photographs from family albums provide a modicum of guidance. Magazines that spotlighted hot rods and customs illustrate many of the finest creations of the 1950s. Before you buy or build a retro rod, a little research is easily and inexpensively done by sifting through the stacks of old magazines at any automotive swap meet.

There are still a lot of the original 1950s-era hot-rodders lurking in the bushes. They have firsthand knowledge of what was on the street and strip. Southern California has always been recognized as the hotbed of hot-rodding, but hot rod roots run all through the United States. In cities, towns, villages, farms, ranches, and lonely rural outposts, hot rods were tops. Like dialects and different ways of waving hello, hot rod styles were regional, demonstrating particular habits and procedures from different areas. It could be favoritism for a particular make of car or engine, a preferred type of exhaust setup, or an approved method of car club identification—such as a plaque in the rear window or mounted below the rear bumper.

A Hot Rod Original

Tom Leanardo of Anaheim, California, is a guy who has been involved in hot rods since the 1950s. He owns a 1932 five-window coupe and a 1936 pickup built in the retro 1950s style, plus he owns several other rods and miscellaneous hot rod parts. Leanardo tells stories about buying these cars back in the 1950s and early 1960s when the 1930s-era cars and trucks cost as little as $20. If you paid $300 that was a lot of money for what most people considered "just an old car."

Leanardo grew up hot-rodding. He picked up cues about how to do it from guys who were building speedsters a

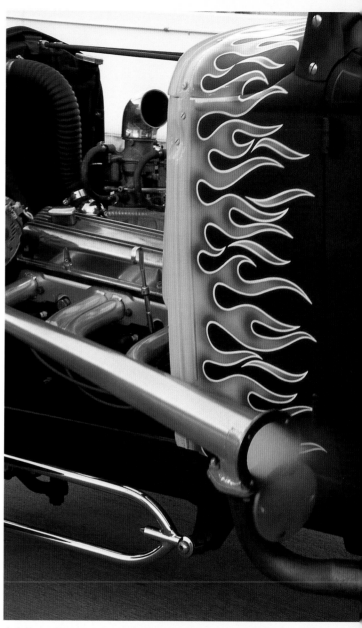

Building a rod according to personal preference appeals to many enthusiasts. Choose whatever steering wheel, instrument panel design, and other accessories you prefer as long as they're not more modern than the rest of your rod.

Adding flames to a rod requires an artist's touch. Styles vary and have evolved over the years along with the paints that are used. With a retro car you don't want to go too far into the future with a paint and flame style.

Many of the original hot-rodders are still involved with building cars the same way they always did. This 1934 Ford sedan, built by Clyde Bangiola, looks like a bone stock factory original, but under the hood is a muscled-up flathead. The extremely rare set of 1930s-era General Jumbo 14-inch wheels are a classy accessory.

generation earlier. His father was a neighborhood pal of hot rod legend Ed Iskenderian and Iskenderian's hot rod friends. Those connections gave Leanardo the opportunity in 1971 to buy an original condition Model T speedster that is a classic prewar hot rod and a virtual twin to the car Elvis Presley drove in the 1957 movie *Lovin' You*. Leanardo has numerous photographs of the car that were taken shortly after the close of World War II that identify many of the unique components, and he can recite the stories of Iskenderian and others who remember the car on the street.

The rod has received some cosmetic attention to restore cracked paint and upholstery, but it remains essentially as it was built. When rodded in 1939, the body was modified very little, with one noticeable feature being a filled cowl. Another popular customizing feature of that era, and the postwar era as well, was dropping in the handsome instrument panel from an early 1930s Auburn. A 1938 flathead with Stromberg carburetors provides the power, and the headers were handmade from Model A exhaust pipes cut and welded together. The wishbone suspension is a neat trick considering it was 1939. Under the skin a cage was fabricated to strengthen the body.

Other items used in this early hot rod were airplane-strut headlight mounts, 1939 Ford taillights, a license-plate light customized from a Mercury, and the front end from a 1936 Ford, which was considered a good idea then. The steering box is from a Willys and the dual-coil set up was from a Lincoln Zephyr. The door handles are from a 1935 Ford.

Leanardo, and many other guys who built and drove their own rods during the 1950s and 1960s, are entertained by and enthusiastic about the younger people who have taken an active interest in retro rods. When he was a kid Leanardo says building hot rods was the cheap thing to do. A generation later, his son builds retro-style hot rods as a business.

Keep Your Eyes Wide Open

Tom Branch is one of the young guys who developed an interest in retro rods. After being involved in hot-rodding for a few years, he became more and more interested in tracking down a car with some hot rod history. It was 1996 when he caught sight of a funky 1970s-style rod for sale at a cruise night in Downey, California. After just one look, Branch realized the rod was suffering from owner neglect and recognized it as an older rod because of the unique hairpin front suspension and a

Twin carburetors on an Eddie Meyer high-rise manifold make sure this Ford V-8 isn't starved for fuel. This beautifully detailed Ford flathead is dressed for show, but it's got plenty of hot rod get up and go.

327-cubic-inch Chevy engine. The car was definitely old school and not the kind of stuff most rodders were into at that time.

After doing a little bit of detective work, he identified it as a *Car Craft* cover car in 1964. At that time it was equipped with a 409, four-speed, slicks, and chrome reverse wheels. He also discovered the car had a movie role as the James Darin car in *The Lively Set*. Even with that interesting past life, the car had more secrets to tell from an even earlier hot rod experience.

Branch tracked down previous owners and found out the car was also on the covers of *Hop Up* and *Hot Rod* magazines in 1952. At that time it had a track nose, Duvall windshield, a Ford flathead, and a 1939 Ford three-speed transmission. It was also exhibited at a car show at the Pan Pacific Auditorium in 1952, one year after it was

This is more proof that a retro rod can fit many descriptions: Only the lowered stance of this 1933 coupe hints at the hot rod beneath. Notice the nice contrast between the apple green wheels and the black primer.

built by a renowned East Los Angeles hot rod and custom shop run by Al and Gil Ayala. Back in the 1950s the Ayala brothers were part of a car club known as the Auto Butchers. Coincidentally, the East Los Angeles car club that Branch belongs to today is the same Auto Butchers club.

By piecing together the rod's past, Branch traced a lifetime of continual alterations. Similar to everything else, fashions change. In the 1960s the track-nose was no longer popular so it was discarded. Not surprisingly, as the car

aged, it suffered the ravages of owner abuse and neglect. When Branch found it, the interior was upholstered in black corduroy. The original instrument panel, a rare Stewart Warner layout called the Straight Eight, was gone and a wood-grain dash had replaced it. Like any restoration project, there were many things requiring attention in order to return the car to something resembling its 1950s origins. The Model A radiator shell was part of the 1970s look that Branch wanted no part of, so he swapped it for a Deuce shell.

There were a lot of home-built rods put together with ingenuity and scavenged parts. In the retro rod world these are the rat rods. Building a rat rod is like preparing a meal with leftovers. There's nothing to say it won't turn out good.

Underneath the body, the wood structure was a vintage 1950s repair of an original wood framework. And although the rod looks cool with its open-hood style and tri-power 327 gleaming in the sun, Branch's desire is to return the rod to its 1951 configuration with a flathead and a quick-change rear end. Like any hot rod or any restoration project, Branch's rod is a work in progress.

Paying Attention to Details

Building a retro rod requires attention to detail just like the restoration of a bone-stock factory original car or truck. Even though a 100 percent authentic job may not be the objective, a few mismatched items can look as out of place as a welder in a French maid's outfit. Most retro rods don't just look the part—they're retro inside and out. Yet some latitude is given if the attitude is there. Occasionally a modern engine or modern automatic transmission is slipped into rods and customs that otherwise are true to their 1940s or 1950s roots. The owners of these cars don't pretend their cars are something they're not. If the rod or custom is otherwise detailed with vintage parts and style, the owner may be cut some slack, especially if he or she is committed to the hobby. Posers, those who pretend to be interested in hot rods, are judged more harshly by the enthusiasts.

Engines and speed played a big role in the original hot rods. The customs were more about show than go, but the engines still were juiced beyond their factory qualifications. Retro rods tend to be drivers rather than racers, but that doesn't mean they can't burn it up. Regardless of the era and the technology, the process of hopping up engines begins with three basic points:

fuel delivery, valve timing, and exhaust.

Multiple carburetors were always one of the first items to get attention when building a rod. Because they sit right up on top of the engine, they make a statement about a rodder's intentions. Maybe you can't judge a gunfighter by the size of his gun, but it's a pretty good indicator of how serious the opponent is.

It was a widely accepted fact that stock engines were starved for fuel. Rods running flatheads and six-cylinder engines always were upgraded to at least two two-barrel carbs, and three, four, and sometimes more were commonly put to

The general guidelines that apply to building a retro rod are also adhered to when working on a rat rod—build it like the rodders would have back in the 1940s and 1950s. This roadster body started out as a 1937 Dodge pickup truck cab. Note the unique headlights and the ´34 Ford grille shell.

use. Stromberg 97s on a Ford flathead were just about as common as packs of cigarettes rolled up in T-shirt sleeves. With the overhead-valve engines, the smaller engines such as the Chevy 283s and 327s often took advantage of the three deuces setup, while the bigger displacement engines (most often more than 330 cubic inches) went with a large four-barrel or dual quads. A few of the high-performance junkies experimented with superchargers, but it was relatively rare on the street.

Working in conjunction with the high-volume fuel pumpers were the high-performance camshafts. Standard cams were designed for operation at fairly tame rpm ranges, but speed equipment companies such as Winfield, Potvin, Iskenderian, and Smith-Jones were well-known for their cam grinds that improved valve timing when the engine was running wide open. At a slow rpm these cams were readily distinguishable by the extremely rough idle. The lopey rumble of an engine equipped with a high-performance cam could generally draw sideways glances from the street racing guys who cruised the local hangouts.

Obtaining more horsepower without showing it has its advantages when it comes to racing. Larger valves and lightweight valvetrain components usually accompany the installation of a performance cam. Porting (opening up the intake and exhaust ports) for more efficient airflow also helps squeeze out a few more horses. Polishing the valves, valve surface area, ports, and chambers are other methods of coaxing more performance.

Higher horsepower is frequently sought through higher compression. The first step in that direction is to mill the surface of the heads. The goal is to obtain a compression ratio of between 9.5 and 10.5 to 1.0. At this ratio, it is still possible to use common premium grade gasoline. The 1949 to 1951 Olds engines can be milled .100 of an inch, which is substantial, but it is more common to mill between .040 and .060.

A sweet-sounding engine was also high on the list of importance. Dual exhausts were a must, and the coolest engine tones came from Smitty's mufflers. Mellow-tones and Hollywood mufflers were also highly regarded for their quality, low-throated rumble, but for performance-enhancing power, headers were the answer. Headers are designed to get rid of exhaust gases faster, and their efficiency could boost horsepower by 5 to 10 percent. The design was either straight pipes or a twisted cluster known as a "bunch of bananas." It wasn't unusual for rodders to manufacture their own headers and the open-hood retro rods that are dressed out with these get extra attention. With a fully exposed engine, headers and a multiple-carb setup were an important signature for any rod.

A rat rod takes advantage of whatever works, might work, and can be made to work. What appears to be random and reckless actually is somewhat methodical. This roadster pickup has logged thousands of miles. The red fuel lines are an authentic 1950s accessory item. This car was built by Jonny Guilmet of the San Diego-based Deacons car club.

Power Packed and Race Ready

Although Ford flatheads power more hot rods and customs than any other engine, the early Oldsmobile Rocket V-8s are probably the next most popular. They came on the scene in 1949 about a month after the first Cadillac OHV engines. Due to their compact size, they were an easy fit for many chassis. Low-end torque, a hot-rodding essential, was their specialty due to a big bore and short stroke. The original displacement was 303 cubic inches. Higher compression heads came in 1952, and Oldsmobile increased the bore in 1955, which took displacement to 324 cubic inches.

A stock Olds V-8 in 1949 was capable of churning out as much horsepower as many of the hopped-up flatheads were putting out, and the manufacturers kept pouring it on. According to Oldsmobile sales literature, from 1949 to 1956 the factory Olds engine increased from 135 horsepower to 202

horsepower. The credit is easily traceable to bolt-on speed parts. Any rodder who had the early Olds engine could easily corral the same horsepower gains by following the same moves the factory was making. In the mid-1950s, when one of the new Oldsmobile 88s was hauled off to the junk yard after a wreck, there was probably a hot-rodder there waiting for it to arrive.

The most potent engines of the early to mid-1950s were the Chrysler hemi motors, including Dodge and DeSoto. The high-performance racing guys were winning

A hand-built tubular steel grille insert provides a distinctive appearance to the often-used 1932 Ford grille shell. Rocket Olds 88 emblems on the sides of the cowl let everyone know what's running this rod.

big with these at the drags and on the dry lakes. Rarely will a retro rod be running one of these, but when one shows up it is guaranteed to attract some serious attention. Although speed equipment was readily available, these engines were always expensive. Big demand and short supply will do that. If you were lucky enough to find one and had the bucks to buy it, then you had to wrestle with the size of the engine. These engines are wide and almost always required some creative cutting on frames and bodies to get a good fit.

The overhead-valve Cadillac engines of the 1949–1951 vintage, much like the Oldsmobiles of this time, are also held in high regard. Packing a Cad engine into a rod was an impressive sight, especially when it was crowned by dual-quad carbs. Cadillac made many performance improvements throughout the 1950s as the horsepower race heated up, and virtually every one of them was easily retrofitted to the original OHV V-8s. The reputation of these monsters was built on ruggedness, dependability, and a decent power-to-weight ratio.

As popular as the flathead Ford engines were for the first 10 to 15 years after World War II, the mid-1950s debut of the Chevy V-8 was a hot-rodding milestone. Prior to the Chevy V-8 most Chevy performance enthusiasts chose the 270-cubic-inch and the 302-cubic-inch GMC six-cylinder engines to get more power than the smaller

Vintage 1958 Chevy taillights are not the typical rod selections, but they are in keeping with the overall 1950s theme this owner has chosen.

Chevy sixes would deliver. The 265-cubic-inch V-8 engines changed everything. The change wasn't immediate, but the ripple effect had begun. After two years the 265 was replaced by the 283. In the minds of many people the 283 was the best engine ever built. It was a smooth-running, inexpensive unit that could be hopped up to outperform engines of much larger displacements. The high-performance aftermarket businesses raced to get a piece of this action. Chevy enthusiasts finally had the punch to go toe-to-toe with Ford. During the remaining 10 years of the classic hot rod era, Chevy slowly took control of the fight.

After the 283 came another great Chevy engine—the 327. In factory Corvette trim or with the Power pack option on a standard Chevrolet, these engines made the term

This roadster is an example of the diversity of cars in the retro rod field. Although it looks like a show car, owner Bill Franey says, "I built it because I want to drive it. If you don't drive it, what the hell good is it?"

This metal-flake blue Deuce roadster is being restored as a 1960s-vintage retro rod. It's brightly painted, uses a lot of chrome, and wears cheater slicks. Radir wheels are a personal preference of the owner and are extremely rare.

factory hot rod commonplace. They were the reason a lot of 1955–1957 Chevys were starting to line up next to the traditional hot rods on the street and at the drags. They also found their way into many of the 1930s-era Ford roadsters and coupes. With the performance technology of the era, these small-block Chevys just flat-out ran like stink. They were the modern flathead because they were plentiful, didn't take a rich daddy to buy, and the hop up goodies were readily available.

Hard on the Gears

Getting the power to the rear wheels was sometimes challenging. During the late 1940s and early 1950s, all rods were shifted with manual transmissions. The choices were floorshifts (mixing sticks) or column shifts (mixmasters). As engines were tuned for higher performance,

drivetrain components started failing faster than shop students in algebra class. Gear jammers gravitated toward transmissions that could take the punishment. The solution to that problem was Cadillac and LaSalle transmissions. These transmissions became junkyard treasures because they had a reputation for being strong and dependable. The floorshift 1939 Cadillac side-shift gearbox had many fans in particular. Cadillac standard transmissions all the way to 1950 were popular among rodders.

Rods running flatheads often ran Ford transmissions and rear ends, but the preferred upgrade was the 25- and 26-tooth

All the manufacturers were engaged in a horsepower race throughout the 1950s, but Oldsmobile really gained a performance-oriented following. As more and more hot-rodders turned to Oldsmobiles for power, the newfound Olds performance image grew.

PREVIOUS PAGE
One of life's little pleasures is a drive from Los Angeles to Las Vegas in a retro-style roadster. This one is parked outside a cafe on Route 66 just outside of San Bernardino, California.

close-ratio Lincoln Zephyr gears. You didn't race too many times before noticing the close ratio gears could make a difference. The loser's lament, "I had him until I shifted gears," could have been remedied with close ratio gearing, which prevented the excessive loss of rpm during shifting and kept the engine in the range for maximum horsepower.

Putting Zephyr gears behind a Chevy engine would make a holy man curse like a sailor. It was an intricate procedure that wasn't cheap. To top it off, these

configurations were prone to blowing up. A better transmission choice for the Chevy enthusiast was to use the 1936–1941 Packard transmissions from the junior series Packards. Not only was it an easy installation, but the gear ratio was similar to the 26-tooth Zephyr box. Old Packard gears were cheap to buy in the mid-1950s and the rodder had his choice of using the 1936–1938 floorshift or the 1939–1941 column shift. Locating gears from a Zephyr or a Packard wasn't that easy in the 1950s. Today it isn't any easier.

In the 1960s reworked General Motors HydraMatics became the first automatic transmissions to gain widespread popularity. Their biggest benefit was the capability to withstand the tremendous torque generated by the high-performance engines. In the early 1950s, anything with more than 150 horsepower was considered a serious hot rod. Ten to 12 years later horsepower had doubled and standard transmissions were subjected to huge loads. Rodders naturally gravitated to those that could take the punishment.

Hit the Brakes

Now that rodders knew how to make the cars go fast, figuring out how to stop a rod was another interesting dilemma. Prior to 1940, Fords used mechanical brakes, which were fine for normal speeds if they were kept in good condition. Only

A no-frills rod couldn't look any better than this. Take a 1932 coupe, strip off the fenders and running boards, lower it, and add some pop under the hood and drop in stylish red and white pleated interior.

Immaculate restorations and recreations of 1950s-era hot rods have led to recognition of these cars at prestigious car shows such as Pebble Beach. The Antique Automobile Club of America has also established a new judging classification for American hot rods.

the reckless built hot rods without upgrading to hydraulic (juice) brakes. It was a frequent upgrade. Therefore, kits were manufactured that allowed juicers to bolt right up to the original spindles.

Brake technology improved dramatically in the 1950s, yet it was considered inadequate when it came to high-performance situations. More than a few people who work on cars of this vintage still don't trust the factory brakes. Those who are not so concerned say the weakest link in the braking system has always been the linings. Modern linings have significantly improved old hydraulic brakes. The debate continues, but the use of hydraulic drum brakes on light vehicles, such as hot rods, does not appear to be troublesome. Those who remain unconvinced won't go with anything less than disc brakes, but they won't win many admirers on a retro rod.

Heat is the enemy of drum brakes, and the 1950s rods sometimes were fitted with finned drum brakes to help cool them off. They are a rare item today and something retro-rodders love. Most were used in racing where the improvements were

obvious. Reducing the temperature around the drums had a direct and positive effect on braking by reducing fade. Other techniques include drilling holes in the backing plates and fabricating scoops that duct air through the brakes. Aluminum drums were an advancement in keeping things cool, but few were made. Buick was one manufacturer that used bonded aluminum brake drums. Retro-rodders have their "parts radar" dialed into these.

Most of the original hot rods were driven hard and put away wet. They were lucky to survive the short-term service requirements they performed, let alone the test of time. It makes the genuine article a rare find and a treasure hunter's prize.

Occasionally a rod is discovered. It may be a 100 percent original hot rod, or it may have suffered through some butchering during its lifetime, so it's hard to identify when it was originally built. Bodies, frames, engines, speed equipment, and assorted accessories are still out there to be found. There is a small but growing number of enthusiasts looking to save those hot rod treasures before they rust away or are thrown in the crusher.

raditionally customs have been about changing the factory appearance of a vehicle. The expectations are to create an appearance like nothing else on the road. Some owners prefer the highly accessorized look and fully loaded their rides with every conceivable item the factory, dealer, and aftermarket manufacturers produced. Other owners chose to strip the car naked, removing every trace of brightwork except for the grilles and bumpers, to come up with a minimalist design that said less is more. Taking the big step from mild custom to wild custom involved extensive metal work to chop the tops, channel and section the bodies, and, in many cases, completely disguise the make and model of the vehicle.

Redesigning stock automobile bodies into custom cars has been rediscovered by today's youth. The customs of the late 1940s and early 1950s are back on the streets again, often piloted by people in their 20s and 30s. Slammed Mercurys, Fords, and Chevys, with that sinister and sensual nonconformist style, are playing a big role in relighting the rod and custom flame.

Like hot-rodding, the early postwar customs have a heritage that is closely aligned with the 1930s and include roots that date back to the early days of the automobile. During the 1920s and 1930s luxury cars were usually the benefactors of talented metal shapers and upholsterers. Cars such as Duesenberg, Packard, Cadillac, and Lincoln—owned by folks with

Up front, the Chevy grille, DeSoto bumper, and frenched headlights work together beautifully to provide a unique appearance for this retro-style custom.

Mercury wears the crown as king of the customs because of the 1949 to 1951 models. There are other great Merc customs and tremendous sleds from across the automotive ranks, but these are the tops.

RIGHT
A radically chopped top and toothy DeSoto grille are two custom touches that give this 1951 Merc the sinister appearance that captures attention wherever it cruises. This particular Merc is in well-preserved original condition.

deep pockets—were given the custom treatment by coach-building companies with reputations established on unique design and excellent metal fabrication skills. But by the end of the 1930s, most of these shops were out of business and this high-brow customizing was seldom seen. These big-dollar customs are highly prized by classic car collectors.

In the late 1940s when the good times began to roll again after more than four years of war, customizing was reinvigorated. This time, however, it was more closely aligned with cars affordable to the working

class. The auto factories were not back to full production after years of producing for the military, and the public was hungry for new automotive excitement. The circumstances provided custom shops with an opportunity to show how they could restyle and modernize used cars into something special. Mid-1930s Fords made particularly good customs, and the most popular of the prewar customs were the 1936 Fords. With a chopped top, louvered hood, dropped front end, ribbed bumpers, and a molded-in Packard grille, this car was (and still is) the bomb. The 1940 Fords were almost as popular as the 1936, although it should be noted that popular is a relative term.

Jon Fisher is a member of the Choppers, a Burbank, California, club. He owns several

Frenched headlights, shaved hood treatment, custom bumper, Buick wire wheels, and Appleton spotlights are all classic elements that make this custom an American icon.

retro-style rods and customs, and one of his cars is a 1936 Ford coupe customized in the early postwar streamlined style. It's a unique design that is influenced by a custom, owned by Jack Calori, that appeared in magazines shortly after it was completed in 1948. Calori's car also started with a 1936 Ford coupe. In customizing his car, Fisher added a 1939 LaSalle grille, and 1940 Buick headlights. Like Calori's car, Fisher chopped 3 inches from the top, which visually added length of the hood. It's raked in the front and dropped in the back "motorboat style." It's a very futuristic style for that era. The taillights have been removed from the fenders and were built into the 1941 Mercury bumper guard.

In addition to having a sharp eye when it comes to recognizing the talent that went into the original customs, Fisher put some of his own ideas into the car. For instance, he liked the look of the Lincoln Zephyr dash and instrument panel. He found the Zephyr dash, which was ultimately used in his custom, lying in the mud at a swap meet. It required some adapting to fit in the Ford, but the result is retro cool.

Maybe other customizers used this Zephyr dash idea and maybe no one did, but Fisher made it work in his car. It fits in well with the overall retro customized look he gave his prewar Ford. Like most other retro rods and customs it shows an attention to detail that is historically correct. He also chose the wheels, tires, steering wheel,

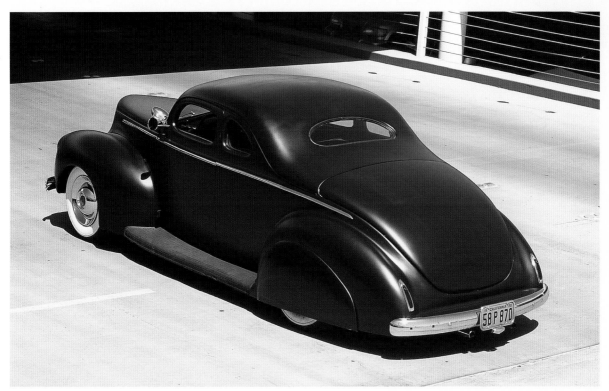

From the prewar era, the 1940 Ford coupes were excellent choices for customizing. The smooth body shape is accentuated by a mildly chopped top and fenders molded into the body.

seats, and the interior and exterior colors based on research about what was being used in the late 1940s. Within those guidelines, Fisher allows some leeway for simply what he thinks looks good.

Another detail uncovered in Fisher's research was moving the gear selector to the left side of the steering wheel, which was done so that shifting could take place without the driver taking his hands off his date. Nice touch. It reminds Fisher of an old saying, "Customs are for gettin' the gals. Hot rods are for forgettin' about the gals."

Moving into the mid-1950s, the used cars most likely to become customs were the 1949 to 1951 Fords and Mercurys. The same vintage Chevys, Cadillacs, Oldsmobiles, Buicks, and Pontiacs were hot custom selections as well, especially the fastback body styles. Most customs were made from five- to eight-year-old used cars, so as the rod and custom era progressed into the late 1950s, the mid-1950s cars became the customizers' favorites. Fords and Mercurys still ruled, but Chevys were a close third. After that it

Most customs were built for looks rather than speed, but some had a lot of hot rod in them. This 1938 Ford is painted in a style reminiscent of the early postwar dry lakes racers. It has recently turned in 140-plus miles per hour on lake-bed runs.

was anything goes with cool tricks being worked on cars of every description.

Low, Lower, Lowest

One of the most difficult customizing techniques was chopping the curved tops that were used on coupes and sedans of the mid- to late 1930s, and the fastback rooflines of the late 1940s and early 1950s. Chopping the top lowered the roofline, usually between 2 and 5 inches, and produced a more streamlined and

aerodynamic shape. The process involved the removal of a section of the roof support posts and the reattachment of the roof on the shorter supports. It was a fairly straightforward operation on vehicles of the 1920s and early 1930s when the roofs were square with the bodies, but as cars became more streamlined and the roof pillars more curved, the chopping process required greater skills to complete it successfully.

Only so much chopping could be done while maintaining an attractive sense of proportion and design. Windshields and rear windows were especially difficult to resize appropriately, and all the window glass needed to be trimmed accordingly when inches were taken from the roofline. Depending on the height of the driver and passengers, adjustments in seats might have been be required to maintain adequate headroom.

Because automotive design always favors a low car when it comes to appearance, the process of channeling a body gained popularity. Nearly all cars are manufactured with the body mounted on top of the frame. When a car is channeled, the body is removed from the chassis and lowered around the frame. To accomplish this task, the floorboards are cut out and the body is lowered down over the frame. Afterward, the body is fastened to the bottom and sides of the frame. There is a direct relationship between how far the body is channeled over the frame and how much higher the floor pans and drive shaft tunnel are positioned when they are rewelded in place. A new seat structure is required to enable the occupants to remain in somewhat comfortable positions since the floor is closer to the roof.

Lowering the body on prewar cars, with fenders separate from the body, brought the fender line closer to the top of the hood and trunk. This accentuated the lowness of the car and gave it a more modern appearance. Some cars can be lowered as

Louvered hoods were a popular touch for both rods and customs in the early 1950s. The roof on this car was already chopped when the current owner found it in the weeds.

much as 10 inches after channeling, which alters their appearance dramatically.

A third customizing method of lowering the body is referred to as sectioning. It is the most difficult to achieve correctly and is accomplished by cutting out a section of the car body below the beltline. In other words, there were two parallel horizontal

These in-fender taillights originally belonged on a 1941 Studebaker. The bumper-mounted taillights were an aftermarket accessory item. DeSoto bumpers were popular because of their ribbed styling.

only did sectioning create a lower profile, it also saved the headroom that chopping the top forfeited. Because of the original slab-sided design of the shoebox Fords, they are perfect candidates for sectioning. The Ford coupes from 1949 to 1951 were high on the list of good-looking customs. Their popularity continues in the current retro trend.

Cars were also lowered in the rear by de-arching the springs and using lowering blocks. Frame alterations such as C-ing and Z-ing were also common. Dropped axles, spindle-dropping kits, and repositioning the A-frame members were used to lower the front of the car. Suspension alterations could lower a car about 3 inches before it changed the ride to farm wagon quality—like the body was welded to the axles. How low could you go was a big challenge when building a custom, and the retro customs are slammed with the best of the originals. Air bag suspensions make it a bit easier today.

When cars are designed and built by the auto manufacturers they tend to have some concern for clear vision in all directions and comfortable seating positions. As a result, there is only so much that can be done to make a production car low and sleek. The customizers were free from such design restrictions because the right look was far more important than comfort. Therefore they could set new standards for cool, and by comparison the

cuts around the car, 3 to 4 inches apart. After removing the cut-away metal, the top and bottom halves of the car were welded together. Moldings frequently hid the seam, but with extra effort the seams were welded and smoothed.

Body sectioning was never as common as chopping and channeling, but when executed correctly it lowered the car and gave it dramatic new proportions that clearly set it apart from the crowd. Not

showroom cars looked tall and boxy. In addition to going low, it was just as important to make a custom unique in many ways.

Dressed to Kill

Fender skirts were practically mandatory on customs. Even though everyone did their own thing when building a custom, few could look the other way when it came to adding skirts. Whether they fit tight in the wheelwell or formed an elongated bubble over the rear quarter panel, skirts were "it" for the customs in the first 10 years or so after World War II.

Behind the skirts rolled big, fat whitewall tires that were barely visible. Up front was another story. The whitewall tires rolled in fully open wheelwells and were capped with the highest fashion in modern wheel disc covers. Although flipper-style wheel covers maintained the popularity they first gathered with the prewar customs, the flipper evolved into the spinner style.

The most sought-after spinner hubcaps belonged to the 1954 Olds Fiestas. The Fiesta was a limited-edition model, so the hubcaps were unique from the beginning. Eventually even the hot-rodders chose them for their cars. The Fiestas proved to be so popular that Olds soon made them an accessory wheel cover for all models. The main drawback to Fiestas was that the hubcaps would not stay on a car long. The combination of better-than-average foot

Tuck-and-roll upholstery was the clear-cut favorite in any early 1950s custom. Chrome window frames are another nice touch.

speed, a screwdriver, and darkness often took its toll. Because the demand continued to outstrip the supply, there are reproductions of the Fiesta spinner available now. A few of the other wheel discs that gained widespread popularity included the 1957 Dodge Lancer, 1956 Plymouth Fury, and the sombrero-style Cadillac models from 1955.

Developing a smooth style was another hallmark of the custom. One of the coolest and most common custom features was the shaved door handles. Handleless doors were

Chopped tops, flames-over-primer paint jobs, wide whites, and cool bullet-center wheel discs are sweet touches for 1949-1951 Ford customs.

operated with strategically placed electric switches that activated solenoids, which "magically" opened doors and the trunk.

Frenched headlights were another almost standard treatment. When headlights are frenched, the headlight rims are welded to the fenders and leaded in so the headlights gain a slightly recessed appearance. After this treatment, any headlight adjustment or replacement unfortunately had to be accomplished from the rear through the fender well.

The same idea was also used on taillights. Manufacturers used taillight design to make a car distinctive at night. A custom car owner wanted nothing to do with brand identity, so taillights were modified or swapped entirely to create a mystery car that had the distinction of being like no other. Fenders were sometimes elongated and molded into the bodies to accommodate these modifications. Taillights from other makes, sometimes cut down or positioned upside down, were often substituted. Almost everything was tried. One of the easiest and most popular swaps for the shoebox Fords was replacing the stock taillights with the bullet-style lights from the mid-1950s Oldsmobile. As the manufacturers made taillights larger and more elaborate, these

Chevy fans can do a lot with the early 1950s bow ties. Extra teeth were added to this Chevy grille, pinstriping replaces factory chrome ornamentation, and Appelton spotlights are mounted on the cowl.

LEFT
A cool chop job gives this four-door 1953 Chevy much improved proportions. Fender skirts accentuate the lowered profile, and shaved door handles add to the smooth contours.

new lantern-like lamps were adapted for custom use on the older model cars. Extending the rear fenders and adapting taillights from a 1956 Chrysler, 1954 Mercury, or 1956 Lincoln each added a unique and handsome style. The most coveted taillights of this era were taken from the 1956 Packard.

The Grille of My Dreams

Swapping the original grilles with the grille (or pieces of the grille) from other cars provided another major step toward distinction, individuality, and personality. The stock grille on the 1949 to 1951 Mercs, one of the most admired customs of all time, were almost always replaced. A reworked 1954 Olds grille was one of the

Tail-draggin' is natural for most customs. The replacement taillights and rear bumper work well to modify this custom's original heritage.

RIGHT
Just a few mild custom touches add distinctiveness to this 1947 Mercury convertible. Note the recessed taillights and license plate. The pinstriping is subtle, as is the lowered suspension.

good-looking alternatives, and mid-1950s DeSoto grilles were also in demand. The vertical grille bars from 1953 and 1954 Chevys were frequently used to customize the grilles of other cars. It was also common to add extra grille bars (referred to as "teeth") to the stock Chevy grille. The DeSoto grilles had a somewhat similar toothy design that was frequently adapted to other models.

When the 1954 Pontiac introduced the floating center grille bar, it immediately became a centerpiece for many customs, especially the 1949 to 1951 Fords and 1949 to 1952 Chevys. Floating grilles were done in many styles, but the effect was a grille bar or grille ornamentation that appeared to be structurally unattached to any framework. It was created by using wire springs and rubber pads. The design actually allowed the grille to rebound when impacted, which provided some degree of damage control.

Smooth . . . Real Smooth

One of the top customizers of that era, Gene Winfield, was fond of adapting 1955 Pontiac front end cosmetics to the customs he built. Winfield's shop was noted for turning out beautiful customs based on the

1949–1952 Chevys. In most cases, the side trim and door handles were removed, and all the holes were filled. Winfield usually replaced the two-piece Chevy windshields with one-piece Oldsmobile units. He also tossed the original grilles, bumpers, and gravel shields. The body panels were either reshaped or new panels were added. To obtain a smooth overall appearance, Winfield preferred to mold in the hood and trunk.

Unique bumper styling was often done with the adaptation of bumpers from other cars and the creative use of bumper guards. The Kaiser three-piece units were a top choice. Good luck finding one today. In keeping with the desired smooth look, bumper bolts were shaved, welded, and filled for a seamless one-piece bumper appearance. Exiting the exhaust tips through the bumper ends was one of many custom styling features

that showed up on factory-built cars several years down the road.

The interiors of Winfield's customs were flashy. The instrument panel was painted and pinstriped or chromed or padded. Chrome plating was frequently added to the window frames, glove compartment door, kick panels, and heater cover. Seats were often recontoured and reupholstered—usually rolled and pleated with one of the new artificial leather fabrics such as Naugahyde. High-contrasting color combinations such as black and white, red and white, or blue and white were commonly selected. The headliners were elaborate and typically matched the seat upholstery material and design. Even the

A low profile and primer paint identifies the starting point for many of the retro customs being built today. In-progress customs are common at the retro rod shows. Spinner-style hubcaps and tunneled headlights indicate customizing intentions.

LEFT
One of the primary ideas behind building most rods and customs was to start with something inexpensive. For the retro custom enthusiast, an early 1950s Mopar is an alternative. Not only can you build a cool ride, but the unique factor goes way up.

interior of the trunk was often finished in matching upholstery.

Many customs were as much hot rod as they were custom. Engines were modified for increased horsepower, some to the extent of building full race engines. Like the hot-rodders, engine swapping was not uncommon. Lake pipes (exhaust pipes that followed the rocker panel area from just behind the front wheel to just ahead of the rear wheel) had great appeal. Mufflers that produced a low, throaty growl, such as Smitty's, were big hits. Tachometers mounted on the steering column were yet another accessory.

By 1959, when the auto companies started building some flamboyant cars of their own, the customizers pushed the limits even further in order to stay ahead. As a result, customs became cartoonish and seemingly the work of science fiction illustrators. Imaginative design was never at a loss, but the world of customs changed immeasurably.

For just about every retro rod being built and those already rollin' down the road, there is a person who belongs to a car club. The clubs are just as retro as the rods and customs that the members return to glory.

Car clubs proliferated in the 1950s. Their names were imaginative creations based on assorted car parts—Piston Jockeys, Hot Heads, and Gear Stretchers; mysterious clans or cliques—Arabs, Sheiks, and Night Prowlers; or gambling and the devil—Black Deuces, Eight Balls, and Lucky Devils. The members showed unity by wearing matching jackets with the club name across the back, and their rods and customs displayed club plaques mounted primarily on the bumpers or various other places.

During hot-rodding's formative years, the local clubs played an instrumental role in popularizing the sport. They provided, at the same time, a unique identity and a team quality; they were like different tribes within a hot rod nation. Each club expressed its individuality with its name and its particular style. While clubs took pride in their uniqueness, they shared a great deal with all the other hot rod clubs. In many areas, the local clubs joined to form larger groups in order to participate in organized racing. There were many such groups, but one of the oldest and most famous was the Southern California Timing Association (SCTA, formed in 1937), that formed the roots of the National Hot Rod Association in 1951.

San Diego–based Deacons hang together once or twice a week. All of the members, except one, are younger than 35 years old. Youthfulness is found among most retro rod club members.

Being a club member requires involvement. It means helping to organize events and supporting the events of other clubs, as well as just hanging out with the guys and turning some wrenches. The cool jacket is just part of the deal.

LEFT
Club identification is noted on almost every retro rod. Most have rectangular plaques the size of a license plate. This cutout style badge is unique. It's not the plaque that makes a club cool. A club's reputation is based on the quality of its cars and members.

RIGHT
The cost of fuel is insignificant compared to the fun of being out on the road with your buddies. This is old-school hot-rodding at its best.

Retro rods are not just a guy thing. Chicks are always involved with the events, which include rockabilly music and swing dancing.

In the early 1950s many states considered laws to prohibit hot rods on the highways. Safety was a big issue due to the home-built nature of the cars and the emphasis on all-out speed. Potentially disastrous alterations to engines, suspensions, and running gear were not uncommon among the mechanically challenged shade tree mechanics. Some of these cars were clenched-teeth and wide-eyed fast, unmistakably dangerous, and driven irresponsibly. What was considered too fast, dangerous, and irresponsible had a wide degree of interpretation; however, it didn't take too many of these hot rod horrors before all rodders were painted with Satan's brush. The outlaw image often cast a nightmarish shadow, especially to those who were bothered by anyone who didn't care for Pat Boone.

Some car clubs promoted the rebel image and pushed it to its limits, others ignored whatever anyone thought about who they were or what they drove, and some even promoted safety and organized racing. Despite the popular perception that hot-rodders were dangerous and out of control, there were clubs that maintained basic safety regulations and car inspections with the idea that hot-rodding could be as safe as anyone wanted to make it.

Midnight racing all the way to Dead Man's Curve, with only one driver coming back to race again makes great movies

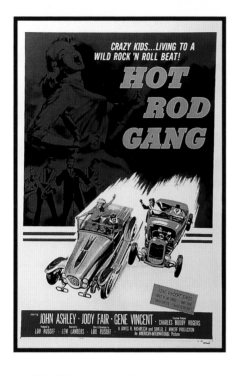

Publicity from 1950s-era films featuring hot rods can be found at almost every show, along with clothing and accessories for those who like to be immersed in the Custom Culture.

and folklore, but those occurrences probably happened less frequently than junior executives crashing their newly purchased fantasy cars right off the dealer showrooms. Stock engines were pumping out much more power than just a half dozen years earlier. Anyone who was young and into hot-rodding at that time will have death-defying stories—wrapped in truth, partial truth, and extemporaneous fabrication—about racing and wrecking. Danger, excitement, and varying degrees of a born-to-raise-hell attitude at times flowed as freely as 19-cents-a-gallon gasoline. It was part of the allure or the abhorrence, depending on your point of view.

Although street racing was important tribal warfare, and speed was status, there were many other aspects to rodding. Reliability runs were popular events that involved completing a predetermined course over public roads within a prescribed time frame. The courses were designed (more or less) to be traveled within the speed limits so high-speed driving was not a winning strategy. The best cars and drivers were able to compete at the closest possible time to a predetermined average speed. Rod runs, often involving many local car clubs, also became popular group activities. Various tests of driving skill were also dreamed up featuring obstacle courses and other

Red and white tuck and roll interiors, luxurious carpets, and ornate, 1950s-era steering wheels are some of the hot accessories found inside retro-style customs.

tricky closed-course routes. Each of these activities prompted participation and friendly competition.

The majority of the local clubs based membership on friendships, neighborhoods, and automotive loyalties. In the 1940s and 1950s, most of the clubs included both rods and customs. There was, in most cases, a mutual respect for each type of vehicle. Membership was granted rather than simply purchased, and club exclusivity was the reward. The same is true with the retro rod enthusiasts. The clubs were small and membership was exclusive. A really big club might have had 15 members, but 6 or 8 were more common. There are many similarities between today's retro rod clubs and those of 50 years ago—the club pride, camaraderie, interaction with other rod and custom clubs, and friendly competition.

The requirements to be a member of the Deacons, a San Diego retro rod and custom club, comes down to two basic qualifications: a common interest in the 1940s- and 1950s-style of building rods and customs and being the kind of person everybody else in the club likes to hang out with. Most of the Deacons, organized in 1977, started out with customs. The reason was mostly economic—a 1950s car is a lot less expensive than a 1930s car. You get more for your money. A young guy without much dough can afford a shoebox Ford or a fastback Chevy in rough condition. It's much

Pinstriping artists display incredible skills, even while people ask them questions and take their photos. Most shows have someone striping cars throughout the day.

easier to find a decent 1950s-era project car for less than $5,000 than it is to find a 1930s car from which to build a hot rod. The condition isn't always a high priority if the price is right; regardless of whether the custom is mild or wild, there is probably going to be some major bodywork done.

Vintage window decals add a little extra flavor. Performance parts, pin-up girls, racetrack memorabilia, and scenic destination decals are popular accessory items that are for sale at most events.

The Deacons started out with six like-minded hot-rodders; four of them had split off from an existing club that had grown too large. "The idea is to have everyone in the club participate," says Jonny Guilmet, one of the founding Deacons. The reason he and several others left their previous club was because they were the core group that did everything together. A club that has nonparticipants is no club at all to their way of thinking. The Deacons hang out together once or twice a week, help each other with their cars, and travel to shows together.

The mainstream car clubs that have dozens, hundreds, or even thousands of members usually rely on a small, core group that does most of the work organizing shows, cruises, and other events. Typically the core members are the ones involved with exchanging technical information and lending a hand with mechanical and restoration problems. The majority of members in a large club go along for the ride. With a large club there are frequently divisions and rifts that work against the collective purpose. Keeping a club small and exclusive to those who want to participate and be involved builds strong club loyalty. "You can't just hand a plaque and jacket to everyone," Guilmet says. "If you just try to build the numbers, and not everyone is friends, it just doesn't work."

No dues. No official meetings. No slackers. For many of the retro rod and custom clubs it's that simple, straightforward, and direct. It's a brotherhood of sorts. Clubs consist of people you can count on and who want to be part of the fun. Member number seven of the Deacons joined about a month after the club first came together, but in the past three years, only two more members were voted in.

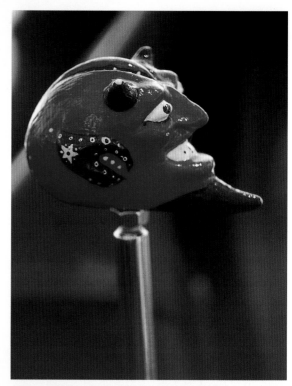

This devil head shifter knob is a cool item, particularly if your club has a name like the Lucky Devils.

RIGHT
This 1932 three-window coupe awaits attention in the shop at the Don Garlits Museum in Florida. Garlits plans to use it as his personal car.

Traditionally rods and customs were built for the street. Building high-dollar versions for show was something that evolved throughout the 1950s and took the hobby in another direction in the 1960s and on into the future. Because retro-rodding is youth-oriented, there is more interest placed on driving than showing what they've built.

PREVIOUS PAGE
The NHRA California Hot Rod Reunion in Bakersfield, California, is a celebration of drag racing history and a destination for many of the highly mobile retro-rodders.

To contribute to the club, it's necessary that the members live close by each other to attend the unofficial regular meetings for garage work or just hanging out. Some clubs have a central garage where members congregate and get most of the work done. One member may have the available space for projects, but things like garage space are fleeting, and shop space for club project cars likely will change. The talents are usually spread throughout the club as well. Even the small clubs probably have at least one member who is skilled at engine work, another who knows bodywork, maybe one member is a painter, or one has special skills that everyone else benefits from. For instance, some guys may not have the mechanical abilities, but they beat the bushes to find the parts that other members need for their cars. The point is that everybody contributes. It's a team effort and the enthusiasm is contagious. "The more you hang out," Guilmet says, "the more you learn about the old stuff and how cool it is. We all have projects in the wind waitin' to be put together."

More than the average group of car enthusiasts, doing your own work is a badge of honor among the retro-rodders. There are clubs where guys are on their own, learning as they go, and some have the graybeard, original 1950s-vintage hot-rodders helping the younger guys figure things out. Guilmet's dad is a hot-rodder from the mid-1950s. He built rods and customs then and still builds them today. Guilmet's father has shared a lot of his knowledge with the Deacons. Another member, Julio Hernandez, is from a family that comprised the Bean Bandits, a truly legendary San Diego–based club that established high-speed records at the drag-racing tracks and on the dry lakes during the golden days of hot-rodding. Guilmet says he and Hernandez were schooled at a very young age on what was right and wrong when it comes to building rods and engines in the retro style.

Several of the Deacons build and drive retro rods that are done in a style known today as "rat rods." They are nearly 100 percent authentic, late 1940s- and early 1950s-style home-built hot rods. These vehicles were built with dry lakes racing in mind. Looks are important, but not in the manner of perfect paint, chrome, and upholstery. Suede primer is the preferred paint of the rat-rodders. If not primer, any

When rods like this first roamed the streets, gas cost less than a quarter per gallon and you bought it at service stations. Now there's little or no service left and the stations charge you 25 cents when you need air in your tires.

In a world where the extreme tends to coexist with the ordinary, wild 1950s-style customs still have the power to make people notice what you're driving. Some things never change.

low-gloss paint that avoids the high-tech look is pretty much within acceptable standards. Flames and pinstriping are often applied on top of primer or in-progress body and paint work. What looks best in this case is a rare part that was discovered in the weeds of a junkyard or during an early morning swap meet raid.

Original hot rods and the right parts to make them truly retro are becoming hard to find. Popular items include 1932 Ford grille shells, Kelsey Hayes spoke wheels, Stromberg 97 carbs, Appleton spotlights, 1937 DeSoto bumpers, and Harman and Collins magnetos. Rare parts are a treasure, and when something like an optional steering wheel from a 1949 Merc convertible can be snatched up for use on a slammed custom, it garners great

admiration among the historically well-versed retro-rodders.

Each club knows other clubs in the area (and sometimes across long distances) that share common ideas about the retro rod way of building and driving hot rods. The small clubs become a large retro rod network. They support each other's shows and cruises and foster a friendly rivalry over cars that they've built, distances they've driven, and rare parts they have discovered. The bottom line comes down to hanging out and having a good time.

Go Cat, Go

Not surprisingly the shows that the retro-rodders support are not the type where car owners sit in lawn chairs next to their beautifully detailed and seldom driven

restorations. Because it's more about participation than perfection, the cars at retro rod shows are likely to be works in progress. Conversations are as often about what's next in the building process, or what parts are needed or have been recently found. Cars in two or three shades of primer, and even in bare metal with the scars of recent metal cutting and welds, are on the road and headed to the next show. Some look like they would be lucky to make it across town much less hundreds of miles.

In southern California, there are retro-rodding events happening pretty much monthly. Individual clubs sponsor one or two each year, and anywhere from between 50 and 150 retro rods and customs show up. The best of the retro rod shows is held each Memorial Day weekend in the small central California town of Paso Robles, located on Highway 101. Retro-rodders throughout the West refer to the annual pilgrimage as simply "Paso." Downtown Paso Robles has a park in the main square where hundreds of rods and customs are spread out underneath tall, shady trees. The streets around the square are also jammed with the coolest rods and customs. Up and down Highway 101 the cruise is constant. Friday night there is a huge parade with thousands of people, mostly locals, lining the streets. The event has become so popular that a second meet has been organized for the Labor Day weekend, and the numbers of rods and customs in attendance is equal to

Young people having fun with old cars is not very common among car hobbyists in general, at least not in the same numbers as the young people who are drawn to the retro rods and customs.

what the Memorial Day event was drawing just a few years ago.

The Paso Robles show began in the mid-1980s when the West Coast Kustoms car club had the idea for an annual get-together. During the past several years the Memorial Day Paso Robles show has grown dramatically, which serves as a gauge for the increasing popularity of the retro rods and customs. The fact that a growing contingent of young people with some sense of hot rod history are fueling this and making it a participatory event is unique within the old-car hobby.

Another major retro-rodding event is Viva Las Vegas, which takes place in March at the Gold Coast Casino and Hotel in Las Vegas. It attracts more than 125 rods and customs, even though it is a grueling drive across the desert to get there from almost anywhere. For the rodders it's a challenge to drive there. The weather is unpredictable and the route includes some long and steep mountain grades.

Retro-rodding is full of challenges and adventures, but the bottom line is still the same as it's always been: hanging out and having fun.

Visually, a couple of cars travel more than 2,500 miles to attend, but the majority comes from a 300- to 500-mile radius of Las Vegas. Once they all converge, the top floor of the Gold Coast's parking garage looks like double-feature night at the Western Sky drive-in theater.

Credit for pulling off this show and mixing it in with a gigantic rockabilly weekend primarily goes to the Shifters, an Orange County, California,-based retro rod club. Viva Las Vegas attracts worldwide attention. It's promoted in Europe, Australia, and Japan, but its content is full-bore Americana. The round-the-clock rockabilly music is a huge attraction for many young kids who are embracing the 1950s nostalgia as a lifestyle that's been labeled "Custom Culture." Music, clothing, art, and 1950s memorabilia are all part of the show. Among the famous attendees at the 2000 show were Rat Fink artist Ed "Big Daddy" Roth, custom car–building legend Gene Winfield, and Paul le Mat, the actor who played John Milner in the movie *American Graffiti*. The famous Milner Coupe, arguably the most recognized hot rod of all time, from the movie was also on hand at the 2000 show.

The big shows like these provide fantastic gatherings of rods and customs;

Although there's no easy way to drive there, car clubs from throughout the West caravaned their rods and customs to the Viva Las Vegas show and rockabilly weekend. The Shifters, from Orange County, California, organized the event.

however, they also shift the attention away from the essence of the hobby and turn it into more of a spectacle. One of the guys from the Choppers car club based in Burbank, California, surveyed the situation at Viva Las Vegas and said, "If there weren't big events being held for the '50s-style rod and custom enthusiasts, the Choppers would just be meeting in a parking lot somewhere on a Friday night to share stories about what they've done or are doing to their rods." It's not about fashion and following a trend. It's all about hanging out and digging these cars.

Although there is a lone wolf and rebellious youth image ingrained in hot-rodding, among the young retro-rodders there is also a strong connection to the history of rodding. Many of the rodders have family ties that go back at least a generation, mostly to fathers who raised

189

There's no shortage of help when car repairs need to be made at a rod and custom show. Viva Las Vegas is one of the West's biggest and most entertaining retro rod shows.

them around hot rods. Vivid childhood memories of riding in Dad's rod are still fresh and, when you ask them, recollections come to mind quickly. Spending time with Dad in the garage made some durable impressions. A father helping his son build a rod for his first car is a story that will be retold many times over the years.

Now the experience is being passed along as another generation is being raised on the old-school rods and customs. They'll have similar fond memories 25 years down the road. There's a far greater family aspect to hot-rodding than a lot of people outside the hobby would imagine. You see it in the frequent picnic-type gatherings that many of the clubs sponsor. As one rodder told me, "You really have to prioritize your life to be able to do this—come to these things and have a care. You make a lot of sacrifices. I got a wife and kids and it gets hard sometimes to do this. When you get really involved, you find the dedication requires a time factor and the money factor."

There's a commitment that affects the whole family, which is probably why it becomes a family activity for those who are really into it. With dedication like that it's not surprising that attention to detail is important to so many.

191

FORD
HOT RODS

DAIN GINGERELLI

ACKNOWLEDGMENTS

As a moto-journalist I'm supposed to maintain objectivity in my work. However, I'm also a hot rod enthusiast, one who harbors unrestrained bias toward traditional-style Ford hot rods. These are the cars that I was exposed to when I was a young boy growing up in the Midwest during the early 1960s. At that time my brother, Alan, and I built and accumulated what amounted to a miniature car show of AMT 3-in-1 model car kits. Many of the model cars we built resembled the hot rods in this book.

Several "car guys"—in their own ways—helped me with this book. Thanks to: Alan Gingerelli; Gary Moline, Tom Leonardo Sr., Tom Leonardo Jr., Nick Leonardo, and their father and grandfather Frank Leonardo for their enthusiasm and friendship; Gene Story for exposing me to hot rods other than traditional-style Fords; Joe Kress, whose editorial insight at *American Rodder* magazine is refreshing encouragement that work should—and can—be fun; and to hot rod magazine editors past and present whose dedication and hard work ensures the longevity of the cars that I truly enjoy.

Thanks also to Al Voegtly, who rummaged through his old scrapbook in search of aging black-and-white photos that showed first-hand the pioneer days of hot-rodding. Also my appreciation to the librarians at the San Diego Automotive Museum (San Diego, California) and the Towe Ford Museum of Automotive History (Sacramento, California).

Furthermore, this book would be incomplete without mentioning my wife, Donna, and our two boys, Kyle and Christopher. Thanks for enduring more car shows and rod runs than you really cared to attend. The three of you are an integral part of my life. Your love and support is beyond description.

Finally, hearty thanks to enthusiasts the world over who enjoy and appreciate a style of hot rod that essentially started the movement that we call hot rodding. Specifically, I thank every hot rod owner whose car appeared in this book; your patience and cooperation is valued.

In memory of Mike Griffin, a thoughtful hot rodder, discreet confidant, and a good friend.

INTRODUCTION

obody in particular invented the hot rod car. Nor can the term "hot rod" be traced to a single source; however, it gained popularity and widespread acceptance in 1948 when *Hot Rod* magazine was first published.

Before that time hot rods were described in a number of ways. As far back as the 1920s hot rodders referred to their cars as "bugs" and "soup jobs." During the following decade, racers on the southern California dry lake beds coined the phrase "hot irons." Later, when the Ford flathead V-8 became a viable source of speed, the hot rods were called "gow jobs," a term that arose from the ongoing feud between owners of four-cylinder engines and the new V-8. The V-8 crowd was fond

Triple A goodness: This trio of Model A roadsters belong to Tom Leonardo Sr., and his son, Tom Jr. The full-fendered '30 in the foreground was purchased by Tom Sr. in 1964 when he was 12 years old. Price: $300. The shiny '29 in the background was formerly owned by noted cam builder, Racer Brown. The primered '31 with red scallops is Tom Jr.'s daily driver.

of saying: "four to plow, eight to gow," thus the expression gow job.

The evolutionary process of the hot rod has its origins before World War I when young men were known to strip their cars of fenders and extemporaneous parts to reduce weight and improve performance. This practice eventually led to organized races, and by the 1930s automobile racing had grown in popularity throughout America, blossoming into a bonafide sport. One of the more celebrated forms of competition was dirt-track racing, taking place on oval-shaped raceways that typically measured between a quarter-mile and a half-mile in length.

As enthusiasm swelled for dirt-track racing, permanent facilities were built to supplement the state fair events. Usually the racing focused on two specialized groups of race cars: open-wheel champ cars and midgets. But a more grass-roots form of racing also emerged during this era. It was the modified dirt-track roadsters.

The modified dirt-track roadsters were, in essence, stripped-down street cars. The most popular were Ford's Model T and, later, the Model A.

Hot rods often were driven by their owners to the race track, where the cars were prepped for competition. By removing the car's fenders and bumpers, the open-top car readily transformed into a nimble (by comparison), lightweight racer.

Beyond those changes, the major difference between a modified roadster and a typical street car was found in the speed equipment under the hood. (That is, if the hood wasn't removed during the car's transformation!) Popular speed equipment for modifieds included multiple-carb intake manifolds, steel-tube exhaust headers, high-lift camshafts, multi-lift valve adjustments, even overhead-valve

Looking much like a hot rod club of the 1940s, the Shifters were formed several years ago, in the spirit of the old days. Club rules state that their cars must be made of steel—no fiberglass—and they must be styled in the traditional manner. "We want rat rods," said one member. "No high-zoot stuff."

(OHV) conversions for the flathead four-cylinder Fords that dominated the class. These modified roadsters helped spawn the early hot rod movement.

About the same time that oval-track racing became a mainstay in America, dry lake bed automobile racing was establishing a foothold in southern California.

The enormous expanse of flat, hard-packed surface made the dry lakes ideal for straight-line racing. And when the racers discovered this phenomena, local race clubs rushed to the desert, promoting their own weekend-long, top-speed contests.

Early dry lake speed events allowed wild hot rod competitions. Sometimes as many as a dozen

Early 1946, and the war is over. Almost immediately hot rodders returned to their cars and racing. Here Al Voegtly (left) and his shipmate Bob Fredricks, stand in front of Al's 1930 highboy. Al was a member of the Clutchers, who raced at El Mirage Dry Lake. Photo by Al Voegtly, Tom Leonardo Sr. collection.

Al Voegtly's 1930 roadster, like many hot rods built during the 1940s, was driven on the street and raced at the dry lakes. It ran 120.96 mph at El Mirage during the October meet in 1948. Photo by Al Voegtly, Tom Leonardo Sr. collection.

hot rods—running 12 abreast—would follow a pace car across the start line. Once they crossed the start line, the speed contest became a free for all. A more refined method was developed by 1938 when the Southern California Timing Association (SCTA) was formed. The SCTA's early format was to allow each car two solo, timed, qualified passes.

The racing became even more competitive when, shortly after World War II, the Crocker Timer was born. Dry lakes racing took on a new dimension as speeds became more precisely measured.

Like their oval-track counterparts, the dry-lakes racers adapted a variety of modifications to their cars to improve top speed. And, like the dirt-trackers, the lakesters stripped their cars of useless sheet metal to minimize wind resistance and reduce weight.

Most of all, these racers tinkered with their engines' parts. As a result the speed-equipment industry grew up and flourished in the region. Men such as George Riley, Vic Edelbrock Sr., Phil Weiand, Kong Jackson, Ed Winfield, Ed Iskenderian, and Eddie Meyer founded speed-equipment companies on the needs of the young racers who hungered for performance.

Automobile racing at this level was pretty much a blue-collar sport. The entry list for both racing venues was comprised mainly of affordable cars like

Plymouths, Chevrolets, and . . . Fords.

Ford would ultimately prove to be the most popular choice. A major factor was the sheer numbers. During the early days of racing, the venerable, lightweight Model T was both plentiful and very affordable. A host of Model T engine performance products was offered by vendors such as Frontenac, Winfield, and Rajo. They helped the new speed-equipment market grow.

The Model A proved just as race worthy as the Model T, even though it was slightly larger and heavier. Because the Model A four-cylinder engine resembled the Model T engine, the speed-equipment industry easily adapted its wares to the new-generation Ford, once again making it a popular choice for racers.

Three members of the Clutchers, a hot rod club formed in Orange County, California, shortly after World War II, pose with their highboy roadsters. The Model A at the left, with its chopped windshield and '32 grille, is a typical example of a traditional hot rod from the period. Photo by Al Voegtly, Tom Leonardo Sr. collection.

A leading builder of high-performance parts during the early years of rodding was Ed Winfield. This pair of Winfield Model S carburetors sit on a Model A engine with a Riley 4-port overhead valve conversion. The engine powers a 60-year-old champ car, currently owned by collector Dick Fitzek.

But what really solidified Ford's presence in hot rod lore was when Henry Ford introduced his lightweight flathead V-8 in 1932. Almost overnight the racers and rodders had an engine that offered more speed potential than the venerable four-cylinder Ford, yet like its diminutive stable mate, the V-8 was affordable. Now the racers—and the pioneer hot rodders who emerged from those dirt tracks and Southern California dry lakes—had access to a powerful, economical engine for their sport.

With the introduction of the flathead V-8, Ford remained an integral part of hot rodding for many years. The flathead Ford became the engine of choice among dry lakes racers and hot rodders, and its four-banger sibling continued to be a popular choice as well. Ford cars were clearly the cornerstone of American hot rodding.

The sport of hot rodding evolved as much from the race track as it did the streets and roadways of America. An example of early racers is this '32 Ford, built by Scott DaPron. He based the car on a similar highboy that his father and grandfather raced at the Gilmore Cup races in 1934.

Early-day hot rodders quite often used military surplus equipment for their cars. This seat is from a World War II bomber. The gloves, leather cap and goggles are authentic 1930s apparel.

Hot rod styles have changed over the years, giving way to a multitude of trends and fashions. Various factors dictated those styling trends. The most notable are: a marked distinction between racing and rodding, the growth and popularity of custom car shows, and the lifestyles and attitudes of the hot rod builders and car owners.

While rodding shared similarities with dry lake and dirt track racing, rodders eventually branched out to other activities such as drag racing, car shows, and reliability runs. By the early fifties, the rift between dirt track racers and rodders had grown even more acute. For that was when dirt tack racing

Sixty years ago there wasn't much of a high-performance aftermarket, so hot rodders used what they could find, such as this tachometer that was built by a company in Stamford, Connecticut.

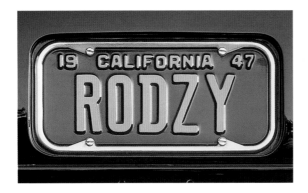

No, they didn't have personalized license plates in 1947. The "Rodzy" plate was fashioned for Mark Morton's 1929 highboy roadster that was styled after a scale-model tether car racer marketed by the Rodzy toy company before World War II.

For many hot rod enthusiasts there's only one car maker—Ford. Manufacturer's tags such as this were attached to firewalls of early Fords.

Only the open-top cars are allowed to park in the main lot during the L. A. Roadsters' annual Father's Day Show. Consequently, you find yourself awash in a sea of drop-top beauty.

became a more specialized sport, even more so than it had during the twenties, thirties and the immediate postwar years. The high cost of racing eventually found its way into drag racing and dry lakes racing, too. And with specialization came higher costs to remain competitive on the track. Consequently, hot rodders unwilling or unable to spend the money necessary to compete at the track dropped out of racing, focusing attention instead to their hot rods' physical appearances and aesthetic beauty.

This shift away from racing also led to the growth and popularity of custom car shows. Chrome parts and flashy paint jobs became hot rodding's trademark in the fifties. By the seventies "Fad T-bucket" roadsters sporting artistic murals and spider-web paint jobs, and tall canvas tops, dominated the scene. By the seventies and early eighties, hot rodding had turned into a fashion statement of sorts.

Eventually, the fad T-buckets and two-tone hot rods (soon to be called "street rods") were supplanted by the "smoothie" look of the eighties. As the name suggests, the smoothie hot rod was a style practically void of extemporaneous chrome parts and protruding pieces. Running boards were filled and "smoothed." Bumpers were removed. Door handles were "shaved." And windshield posts and mirror stanchions were painted to match the body.

One styling treatment has remained an integral part of hot rodding. Rodders today refer to this style as the "nostalgic look," the "timeless look," or the "traditional look."

While there are no specific rules to dictate what the traditional look should be, most rodders agree on several points about "the look." Foremost, it should be timeless. When you look at the hot rod, you should not be able to discern whether it was built five days ago or five decades ago. Second, a true traditional hot rod should be based on a Ford. Not just any Ford, but one that was offered by the Ford Motor Company back in the early days of rodding.

That means it should be a Model T, Model A, Model B, or in some instances Fords produced between 1933 and 1941, and in extreme cases the "fat-fendered" Fords built during the immediate postwar years. Finally, a traditional hot rod should be powered by a Ford engine—either an early-era flathead four, or the more popular flathead V-8. (Non-Ford engine swaps are acceptable if executed in a "traditional" fashion.)

These are the rules as dictated by the purists. But since we're talking about hot rods, we owe it to ourselves to abide by the number one rule of rodding, which is: In hot rodding, there are no rules.

A catch-22 or a contradiction? Not really, because for the most part this book will emphasize three models of Fords—the Model T, Model A and Model B—with a chapter devoted to later-year Fords that are considered part of the original "traditional" movement. Furthermore, we won't restrict our attention to Ford-only powertrains. Some of the feature cars might have non-Ford engines, transmissions, even rear ends. Many of these hybrids are powered by Chevrolet small-block V-8s which, ironically, is the motor that displaced the Ford flattie V-8 as hot rodding's favorite engine.

But throughout this book one thing remains constant about the hot rods featured on these pages. All of the cars were either originally built 40 to 50 years ago or they were recently constructed basing their styling cues on traditional hot rods. Consequently, from curbside every hot rod in this book maintains an appearance that you could have seen on the streets or at a dry lakes meet back in the mid-forties or early fifties. It's a styling treatment that is, indeed, timeless.

Some enthusiasts, however, will argue that the traditional look is more than a timeless style. They contend the traditional look is matchless. Because, for them, nothing is finer than a traditional Ford hot rod. Those enthusiasts also will be the first to say with conviction: "Ford hot rods are forever!"

The 1997 show celebrated the L.A. Roadsters' 40th anniversary as a club. The '97 show happened to be the event's 33rd edition. Other than a brief hiatus near the beginning, the show and swap meet has been held every Father's Day weekend since 1960.

CHAPTER 1

Model T: 1908–1927

PLENTIFUL, AFFORDABLE, MODIFIABLE, RACEABLE

I t's safe to say that the Model T Ford is the land-mark car of the twentieth century. No other car—not Volkswagen's "Beetle" nor any Chevrolet, made a more profound impact on the motoring public than the Model T managed during its 19-year production run.

It wasn't by accident that the Model T became the Industrial Revolution's automotive sensation. Henry Ford had decided from the get-go to build a car for the masses. Practically from the moment that Henry Ford regained control as major stockholder of the Ford Motor Company in 1906, he decided the Model T would be a car that could tap into the low-price market. It was a market segment that, at the time, was pretty much neglected by the auto industry. Henry Ford described the new Model T as a "universal car."

Despite its show-quality finish, Bill Nielsen's modified T resembles those built during the thirties. The body is based on the front section of a 1927 Ford touring, the four-cylinder engine from a Model A. Retro features include a reproduction Winfield head and a custom-made frame. The 16-inch, Kelsey-Hayes wheels are indicative of the period too.

A driver's-eye view lets you appreciate how the modified roadsters were able to cheat the wind. This 1927 T was narrowed 8 inches.

Prior to 1908, when the first Model T rolled off the Ford Motor Company assembly line, America and the rest of the world stubbornly clung to the past, with one foot still in the stirrups of the Horse Age. The Model T helped us out of the saddle, so that we could take the all-important second step into a new era that included machines to assist us in our everyday work and recreation.

You can thank Henry Ford, more than anybody else, for that step into the machine age. Because it was Henry Ford himself who determined that the new car should be simple in design. He also decided to make it lightweight, make it reliable, and perhaps most important of all, to make it affordable. Had there been a crystal ball on Ford's desk, he probably could have added, "And we'll make a lot of them."

History proves that Ford did exactly that. According to records, exactly 15,007,003 Model T Fords were built. It turned the aspiring Dearborn, Michigan-based automobile company into the industrial giant that it remains today.

To truly appreciate the Model T's impact on the auto industry 90 years ago, keep in mind that from 1903 to 1907 Ford had already bombarded the public with a sequence of "letter series" cars. Most of the Fords built during the early years— from the original Model A to the Model S—had sold well. Within four years after incorporating in 1903, the Ford Motor Company had established itself as an industry leader. The Model T reaffirmed the public's confidence in the Ford Motor Company.

Another way to visualize the Model T's influence on American society is to look back at the country's population during that time. By the turn of the century the census indicated slightly more than 76 million people living in the United States. That figure grew to 92 million by 1910, two years after the Model T was launched. And by 1927—the Model T's final year of production—the census figure had swelled another 30 million. When you factor in 15 million Model T Fords to the equation, you realize the popularity that the car enjoyed with the American public and the effect it had on the economy.

But beyond its impact on the general buying public and the U.S. economy, the Model T also had a major influence on the growth of the hot rod industry, which was in its infancy by 1920. That's because the Model T's availability worked in favor of early-day hot rodders and racers who, even like many of today's racers and rodders, made a habit of keeping one eye on the pocketbook whenever they modified their cars.

Within a few years of the Model T's introduction, racers realized the economic potential the car had to offer. Foremost, the Model T was affordable. And once speed-equipment manufacturers began

Chris Fuller set out to build this 1927 highboy roadster more than 20 years ago, when he was 11 years old. It's authentic early-Ford, right down to the 1932 frame, steel body, shortened 1932 grille shell, and 1940 Ford rear end with Halibrand quick-change center. The flathead V-8 has Edelbrock heads and manifold, and genuine cast-iron Fenton headers.

Dennis Love's 1927 looks just as tasty parked on the side of a country road. The car was built for less than $8,000.

developing low-priced aftermarket components for the Model T, that availability spilled over to the race track, where Model T racers were able to compete against more expensive, and more exotic, racing equipment of that era.

Consequently, the racing activity opened the door for a new aftermarket parts industry geared especially for the Model T. Within a few years names like Frontenac, Roof, Winfield, Riley, and Rajo could be found inscribed on high-performance parts destined for "Tin Lizzie" race engines. The conversion parts manifest for the 176-cubic-inch flathead engine—producing a whopping 20 horsepower in stock form at its zenith in 1927—included overhead-valve and dual-overhead-cam (DOHC) heads, high-compression flatheads, multi-lift valvetrains, even big-spark magneto ignitions. Inside the motors lurked hi-po parts, too. The manifest included high-lift camshafts, pressurized lubrication systems, and stronger clutches.

Stronger connecting rods that improved lower-end lubrication were offered, as were counter-balanced, five-bearing crankshafts. The Ruckstell Manufacturing Company even made a two-speed axle to improve the Model T's acceleration and top speed.

Most of the early "speedware" was produced in the Midwest, including parts from Rajo—an acronym that combined the first letter of Racine (Wisconsin, where the parts were built) and Joe (Jagersburger, the man who made the parts)—and Frontenac (ironically, a company formed by two of the Chevrolet brothers, Louis and Arthur; the company was based in Indianapolis). Perhaps two of the more familiar names of aftermarket parts suppliers from the West Coast were George Riley, who produced some of the more efficient cylinder heads and valve assemblies for the Model T four-cylinder engine, and Ed Winfield, a man who developed many exotic camshafts and intake systems for the venerable motor.

Howard Holman bought this modified-T roadster for several thousand dollars in 1990, then he spent several months and a few more bucks restoring it. The suicide front end was common on modified roadsters. Unlike early modified roadsters that usually were powered by Ford fours, Howard's bobtail T has a late-model Pontiac four-banger engine.

More than not, dirt-track racers in the fifties viewed E. "Rosie" Roussel's 1925 Model T from this angle. The powertrain is authentic roundy-round (slang for circle-track racing) too: a Model B Riley four-port motor, in-and-out transmission, and Warren quick-change with locked rear axle.

Even though the Model T's in-line four-cylinder engine was simple and crude by today's standards, it formed the basis for some interesting hop-up items. An obvious place to improve performance was the L-head. One popular overhead-valve conversion was the Laurel Type B, which used 16 valves—four valves per cylinder—to improve the Model T's breathing. Actually, the Laurel head was intended for touring applications. According to the company's advertisement, the Laurel Type B was "the last word in power, smoothness in operation, hill climbing ability, economy and general all around efficiency."

Other cylinder head conversions were offered by Frontenac, which included an overhead-valve (OHV) design by C. W. Van Ranst (the man who also was responsible for the development of the front-wheel-drive Cord and Packard). One of the more sophisticated designs was Robert Roof's 16-valve OHV head that was based and marketed in 1918 as "Peugeot Type Cylinder Heads for Fords."

Aftermarket carburetor kits were offered by Zenith and Ed Winfield, among others. Zenith developed a multiple-carb system that adapted to several of the high-performance cylinder head conversions, and Ed Winfield was noted for his popular Model S downdraft carburetor for the Model T. These and other hot rod conversions helped make the Model T popular both on and off the race track.

By 1923 the racing success of the Model T led to the Barber-Warnock entry in the Indianapolis 500. This car, sporting a specially made "speedster" body that was offered by one of many coach builders in the Midwest, wasn't a typical Model T. But it was, nonetheless, at heart a Ford Model T.

The Barber-Warnock racing engine was equipped with a Frontenac SR overhead-valve conversion with a Winfield carburetor. The car was driven to a fifth-place finish by L. L. Corum. Ahead of the Model T-based speedster was a quartet of Millers, considered one of the premier purpose-built race cars of that era. Not bad company for a production-based car that cost less than $300 off the showroom floor!

Despite the success of the Barber-Warnock Indy car, this and other Ford entries are overshadowed in history by the factory-Ford effort of 1935 that showcased the new flathead V-8 in a Miller-based chassis. Four team cars were entered for the prestigious race, with Ted Horn, who completed 148 laps, placing 14th in the race, highest among the Ford-Millers. (In 1933 Ford dealer C. O. Warnock entered his own V-8-based special, but it failed to qualify. The following year the car, revamped and entered as the Detroit Gasket Special, finally qualified for the 500 — with the third-slowest time. Ironically, the Detroit Gasket Special blew an engine gasket, and the entry was credited with 110 laps. A second Ford V-8-powered entry in the 1934 race was the Bohnalite Special. It launched over the wall and into obscurity on the 11th lap of the race, without serious injury to driver Chet Miller or his mechanic, Eddie Tynan.

Beyond its racing endeavors, the Model T became a mainstay among hot rodders based on two key factors: price and availability. In its first year of production the Model T sold for $550, a bargain at

A popular fiberglass replica Model T bucket was offered by Cal Automotive in the sixties. Several years ago Ron Bertrum was fortunate to locate a basket kit with this body. He restored the T-bucket, and then dropped in a 243-cubic-inch flathead V-8 for power.

Most early flathead V-8 intake manifolds housed a pair of two-barrel carbs. Another popular treatment was the tri-power, or three carb design. This particular four pot—meaning that it holds four carburetors—Edelbrock is evidence that hot rodders have always believed that more is, indeed, better.

the time. By 1924, the height of Model T production, a customer could walk into a dealership with $290, and drive out with a brand new, all-black Model T runabout roadster.

To truly appreciate the Model T's impact on the U.S. populace, it's worth comparing the car-to-population ratio in 1902, when the American automotive industry was in its infancy, with 1909, one year into the Model T's 19-year production run. According to 1902 automotive records, there was one car for every 1.5 million people in America. Within two years the ratio had shrunk to one car for every 65,000 people.

This tremendous growth led *The Nation* newspaper to predict in 1907, "As soon as a standard cheap car can be produced . . . that does not require mechan-

ical aptitude in the operation and that can be run inexpensively, there will be no limit to the automobile market." On March 19, 1908, the public was exposed for the first time to the Model T Ford. And, thanks in large part to the affordable Model T, the ratio of cars to people in 1909 had diminished to one car for every 800 people.

Despite the extraordinary number of Model Ts built, the car was not considered a technological leap forward based on auto industry standards of the time. In fact, the Model T was considered somewhat a comical piece of machinery by many Americans, which accounted for the little Ford's many nicknames, among them "Tin Lizzie" and "Flivver." Fact is, the Model T was the focal point of more than a few jokes during its reign as top-selling car in the world.

One popular witticism went like this:

"What does the Model T use for shock absorbers?"

"The passengers."

After about 10 years of production, even Ford dealers realized the Model T was trailing the rest of the automobile industry in terms of on-road performance and comfort. They begged Henry Ford, who ran his company with authoritarian rule, for a replacement car. Ford, who loved the Model T as he would his own child, responded coolly, "The only trouble with the Ford car is that we can't make them fast enough." (Henry Ford's original goal was to manufacture one Model T every minute; by 1925 the factory was rolling one out the door every 10 seconds!)

And so production continued at the Highland Park facility in Michigan. Despite the Model T's agrarian design, it accounted for 57 percent of all cars sold in the country during 1923. But by 1925 Ford sales were down to 45 percent of the market. Finally realizing that the Model T had outlived its usefulness (in terms of sales), on May 4, 1927, Henry Ford reluctantly announced to the world that his beloved car would conclude its life after the model year; a replacement would be offered for 1928. A few weeks later, May 26, Model T number 15,000,000 rolled off the assembly line.

Years after the Model T production had ceased, Henry Ford was said to have told an associate, "The only thing wrong with that car was that people stopped buying it."

But Ford was wrong. Long after the Ford Motor Company ceased production of the Model T, hot rodders began buying used Tin Lizzies by the thousands. In used condition the cars were

The heartbeat of "Rosie" Roussel's track-T racer is this Model B Ford four with Riley four-port conversion. This motor remained popular for racing until the time of the overhead-valve V-8s of the fifties.

Frank Mack built this 1926 lowboy in 1950. The car was well known throughout the Midwest, and it won Best Hot Rod at the 1953 Detroit Autorama. Mack built the entire car himself, even forming the belly pan. The motor is a modified Mercury flathead V-8.

extremely cheap, offering a young man an affordable set of wheels. Some used Model Ts in the 1930s were practically given away, selling for only a few dollars. With the variety of high-performance parts produced for racing during the previous decade, the Model T made a very attractive starting point for someone interested in building a hot rod.

The Model T remained so popular among hot rodders and nonhot rodders alike that even as late as 1949 more than 200,000 were still registered and on the highways of America. Its popularity carried through to the 1960s, when hot rodding matured into the hobby that it is today. This popularity spawned a market for replica Model T bodies made of fiberglass. The glass bodies offered the same compact, shapely design of an original Tin Lizzie roadster body, but the builder didn't have to worry about repairing corroded metal body panels or plugging bullet holes (many abandoned Model T bodies were found in fields where the Flivver was used for target practice). One of the first aftermarket, fiberglass bodymakers was Cal Automotive, which produced a replica of the 1923 roadster, complete with turtleback deck and trunk lid.

When the hot rod mail-order boom of the mid-seventies began, the industry once again was rife with Model T aftermarket parts. Today companies such as Total Performance in Wallingford, Connecticut, and Cal Custom Roadsters in Anaheim, California, offer parts and complete Model T kit cars to the hot rod public.

Most modern fiberglass replica Model T bodies are based on the 1923 roadster. These fiberglass bod-ies are generally two-piece kits that have either the turtleback or a shortened pickup-bed rear section. They are commonly used for building nostalgia T-buckets and Fad Ts that were so prevalent in the seventies. Replica bodies based on the 1926–27 Model T roadster bodies are one-piece turtleback only. Generally the 1926–27 is considered to be more modern in appearance than the earlier Model Ts. Most often they are used for building Track T or highboy roadsters.

Due to the current boom in reproduction aftermarket "rodware" for the Model T, it's rather easy

In this picture, taken in 1992, the cockpit of Frank Mack's 1926 retains its original look, right down to the cracked, maroon leather upholstery, fat-faced gauges, and the huge three-spoke steering wheel. Hot rod collector Bruce Meyer recently bought and restored the Mack roadster, maintaining its original charm in the process.

to build a complete car using original and mail-order components. Many of the traditional-style Model T hot rods are based on the T-bucket "Kookie Kar" concept that rod-builder Norm Grabowski conceived 40 years ago for the television series *77 Sunset Strip*. But rather than using super-charged big-block engines that sprouted on the Fad T-buckets of the seventies, the traditional Model T-based hot rods favor early Ford motors, including the Model A and Model B four-bangers, Ford's popular flathead V-8, as well as late-model OHV four-cylinder and V-8 engines.

The remainder of the drivetrain usually is based on early Ford hardware, and the suspension is formed around Model A transverse buggy springs, or custom-fitted coil-over shock absorbers. Solid brass Model T radiator shells are acceptable, but most traditionalists today prefer to use a cut-down grille and radiator shell from a '32 Ford. And while the sophisticated four-bar linkage is more practical for aligning the front and rear axles, die-hard rodders usually insist on hairpin radius rods or split wishbones for their cars.

In any case, practically all of the traditional-style Model T hot rods today evoke the spirit of the car that prompted the aftermarket movement so many years ago. Even though hot rodding wasn't Henry Ford's original intent for the Model T, there's no disputing that his Tin Lizzie has become an integral part of the traditional hot rod movement today.

A popular update was to slip a Model A or Model B four-cylinder in front of a Model T body. This modified roadster carries a Model A engine with Winfield head and carbs. The body is a narrowed 1927 touring.

Gabby Garrison built this 1925 Model T based on one he owned in 1933 when he went to Long Beach Poly High School. The roadster has been lowered front and back. Nineteen-inch Buffalo wire wheels replace the stock wood-spoke wheels. The windshield is cut and slanted. "We called them Fords, not Model Ts, back then," said Gabby, "and hot rods were soup jobs."

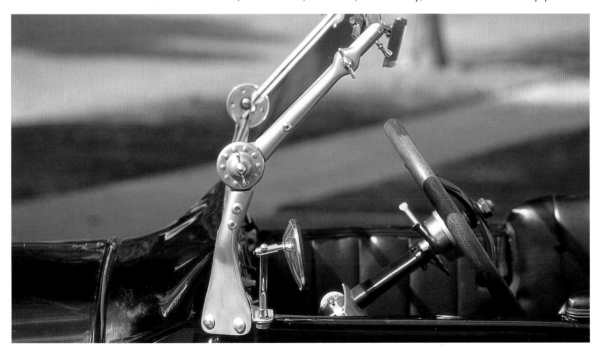

Streamlining? Well, yeah, sort of. Wing nuts allow this shortened windshield to fold back. It can also be folded completely forward "so the wind could hit our faces," according to owner Gabby Garrison who built his first Model T hot rod in 1933.

Home Brew Tub

It's because of guys like Steve Wickert that hot rods evolved in the first place. Working on a tight budget, Wickert built his hot rod for less than what some collectors today would pay for an authentic set of Eddie Meyer heads and manifold. Wickert, who lives in Prescott Valley, Arizona, started the project in 1995, accumulating parts for a car that he didn't own yet.

"I was going to build a Chevy-powered hot rod," Wickert said, however, after attending the 1995 Antique Nationals, he changed his mind. "I saw how much fun they [the participants] were having, so I sold the Chevy stuff and bought the V-8-60."

Wickert happens to be handy in the machine shop, so to cut costs he whittled and shaved and filed the V8-60 block and

Steve Wickert's two-door phantom phaeton started out as a four-door sedan. It ended up as a cool hot rod.

Shown here at the 1997 Antique Nationals, Steve Wickert's $1,200 hot rod launches off the line at Los Angeles County Raceway for a 20-second pass.

heads himself until the engine was like new. To boost performance, he ported and relieved the old L-head block, and milled the heads for more compression. He also gave the little motor a 3/4-race camshaft, and stacked a single Stromberg 97 carburetor on a stock manifold. He fabricated the exhaust pipes himself, forming the steel tubing into the same relative shape as legendary Fenton exhaust headers. Finally he painted the engine red, using aerosol spray paint from the local auto parts store. The remainder of the hot rod's drivetrain is old-timie Ford running gear.

In the meantime, he kept his eyes open for a cheap buy on an old Ford body and frame. He located a shot-up Model A four-door sedan that was abandoned in the desert. Once he retrieved the sedan, he decided to chop off the top and convert the body into an open-top phaeton.

"I sawed off the top, then filled in the rear doors," Wickert said. He plugged the bullet holes and when viewed from curb-side the old sheet metal doesn't look too shabby. "If you look from the inside," Wickert confides, "you can still see where the bullet holes were."

After patching the body he put new sheet metal in the floors, ran a strip of padding around the top edge where the sedan's window garnish molding used to be, then coated the semi-straight body with red primer. Once the car was running, he set off for Palmdale, California, home of the Antique Nationals, in search of fun and good times. Wickert said that the project set him back $1,200, start to finish.

Speaking of finish, the car isn't a slouch at the drags. It posted low-20-second ETs through the quarter-mile at Los Angeles County Raceway. Not bad for a tiny flattie that breathes through a solitary Stromberg 97.

But low ETs or a low price tag isn't what this hot rod is all about. Instead, what sets Steve's hot rod apart from most others is that it represents the spirit of hot rodding as it was so many years ago.

CHAPTER 2

Model A: 1928–1931

TIMELESS STYLE, ENDLESS POSSIBILITIES

W hile the Model T was introduced to the American public at the most opportune time, Ford's timing with the Model A couldn't have come at a worse moment in automotive history. For the Tin Lizzie's replacement not only had some big shoes to fill—up to the bitter end the Model T maintained respectable sales figures—it faced stiff competition among other auto manufacturers who had, by 1928, gained a strong foothold in a market that for more than a decade was dominated by the Ford Motor Company.

By 1928 two other automobile companies emerged as FoMoCo's primary antagonists in the battle for sales supremacy. Leading the assault was General Motors, makers of the low-cost Chevrolet

Another A-V8 that Tom Leonardo Sr. managed to rescue and put back on the streets is this 1929, originally built in 1940 by the late Herman LeHam. The car is a treasure trove of prewar hot rod craftsmanship. Its mechanicals include a 1939 gearbox and rear end, Ford hydraulic brakes, split wishbones, and 16-inch, Kelsey-Hayes wheels with wide whitewall tires. The more rounded '32 Ford grille shell has always been a popular addition to Model A hot rods.

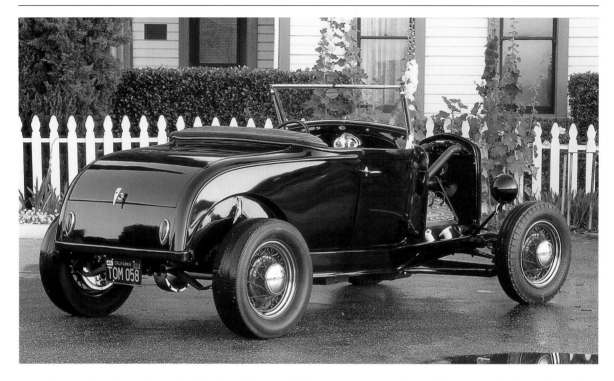

Speculation is that this A-V8 was built back in the 1950s by former moto-journalist and famous camshaft grinder William "Racer" Brown. After acquiring it in 1990, Tom Leonardo Sr. freshened it up, while maintaining the original parts. Most of all, Leonardo got the roadster running and back on the road, "where it belongs," he added.

line. GM and Ford were joined in 1925 by a relative newcomer, Chrysler Corporation. In fact, by 1927 Chevrolet had, for the first time ever, surpassed Ford in sales. Fuel was added to the fire in 1928 when the upstart Chrysler Corporation introduced its Plymouth line, giving the low-price market three strong players. Ford reluctantly moved into a two-front sales war.

Ford readied for corporate combat in two ways. First, it shifted its production to the new River Rouge plant, a huge facility where raw materials were fed in one end of the factory, and a complete car rolled out the other side. The River Rouge plant's main purpose was to produce the new Model A. Powered by an all-new four-cylinder engine, the Model A moved to the sales front October 21, 1927.

Tradition continues to roll, this time using Firestone 5.60-16 sprint car tires mounted on bent-spoke Kelsey-Hayes wire wheels. Although the rib-tread tires often were referred to as "farm implement" tires, they were actually developed for sprint car racing.

Being the first new-model Ford introduced in nearly 20 years, the Model A sparked immediate interest among the U.S. motoring public. Within 36 hours of its introduction, 10 million people nationwide had stopped by Ford dealerships to inspect Henry's new baby. In New York City alone, Ford dealers accepted cash deposits from 50,000 eager customers ready and willing to sample the new car.

The novelty quickly wore off however; shortly after the Model A debuted, Chevrolet announced that a six-cylinder engine was in the offing for its low-cost model line. This news, of course, detracted from the Model A's initial sales, and by the 1929 model year Chevrolet had gained more than a 20 percent share of a market that totaled 5,294,000 cars. Ford had, nonetheless, regained control of the sales war—about 34 percent of the market—with 1,851,000 units sold. As events unfolded, however, that situation would change. (In any case the Ford family, which privately owned the auto company in those years, could have survived even a more drastic reduction in sales. The family fortune in 1926 was estimated to be $1.2 billion—all a result of the Model T's resounding success.)

Few rodders are more enthusiastic than Jim Richardson, shown here taking his 1929 roadster for a spin. The little runabout has a Model B engine with Cragar OHV conversion, and "all the authentic stuff inside to give it more than the original 50 horsepower!" said Jim. The remainder of the drivetrain includes a Model B transmission with Zephyr 26-tooth gears and a Halibrand quick-change rear end.

For a living, Mike Armstrong grows olives on his farm in Porterville, California. And for fun, Mike drives around in this 1931 A-bone coupe that has a Model B engine with Cragar overhead conversion. The 212-cubic-inch displacement engine is fed by a pair of Stromberg 81 carbs. The 1932 transmission has 1939 gears, and the rear end is a 4.11-ratio two-speed Columbia.

But Chevrolet's six-cylinder engine was only one obstacle that the Model A had to overcome in the sales market. Economic disaster loomed over the horizon for the entire industrial world when the stock market collapsed October 29, 1929. Black Tuesday, as that catastrophic day was called, marked the beginning of an economic depression that would last throughout the subsequent decade. With the economic depression came a reduction in the number of potential new-car customers, and by the end of 1933 total new-car sales in the nation peaked at only 1,848,000. During the initial four years of the Great Depression one out of three auto makers had dropped along the wayside, and with them many of the parts vendors who kept the industry's assembly lines stocked with parts.

These economic conditions, of course, were not foreseen by Henry Ford and his son, Edsel, who had been named president of the company by his father about the time the Model T abdicated as the FoMoCo's bread-and-butter winner. As chairman of the board, Henry Ford still influenced company policy, but to his credit he allowed Edsel to oversee the design of the Model A.

Fortunately for the Model A project, Edsel was a man who appreciated art and high fashion. Consequently, when he and the Ford stylists took pencil to paper to design the Model A's sheet metal and interior, they did so with a newfound conviction to produce a car that would, once and for all, shed the plain-Jane, even agrarian, reputation that the Model T had harnessed onto the Ford Motor Company's name. Consequently, while the Model T looked square and stodgy, the Model A—for the first time in Ford's history — came across as a svelte,

Above and Right
Manny Betes built his A-V8 "back in '38 or '39, I can't really remember," he said. In any case, he and his brother, Frank, raced the car—it's little four-cylinder engine bolstered by a Riley four-port conversion—at Muroc (1941) and Rosamond (1942) dry lakes. Manny went the fastest at 107.52 miles per hour. The car is, for the most part, all original, right down to the black lacquer paint!

even stylish, automobile. Gone was any resemblance to a horse-drawn buggy. What rolled off the River Rouge assembly line was a car that looked like, well, a car!

Shortly after the Model A debuted, Henry Ford commented to the press that if there was one thing his son, Edsel, understood, it was style. As proof, he turned everybody's attention to the new Model A. The buying public obviously agreed, as the Model A accounted for more than five million sales during its four-year life span.

Foremost, the Model A lacked the "spindly" appearance of the Model T. The new car sprouted stylish bumpers and contoured running board aprons for a more refined appearance. Furthermore, its larger, more curvaceous body was adorned by wider, yet sleeker, fenders. Its appearance was more up-scale, too, thanks to the chromed radiator shell.

The Model A's interior broke new ground for FoMoCo cars, too. Biggest news of all was the spacious seating for driver and occupants, a treatment that was inherited from Ford's acquisition of the

Lincoln line of luxury cars. The new Model A also had a floor-mounted hand-shifter to operate the new three-speed transmission, and a more thorough array of instruments were positioned in the center of the dashboard. Topping off the interior was a new 21-inch diameter steering wheel that was in sharp contrast to the Model T's inverted wheel, a carryover from the automobile industry's infancy.

Interestingly, the designation Model A broke tradition with Ford's policy for naming new models. From the first Ford through the Model T, each subsequent model name had been determined by the next letter in the alphabet; thus, Model B followed the original Model A, C followed B, and so forth. By rights, the 1928 Model A should have been termed the Model U, however, Henry Ford was so taken by the demise of his beloved Model T, and he harbored such high hopes that its successor would breathe new life into the auto company, that he christened Edsel's car after FoMoCo's first automobile, built near the turn of the century. And so, Model A it was. This turn around also was a tribute to Edsel in certain ways, marking the beginning of what appeared to be a new era for the largest automobile company in the world.

Not only did the Model A boast new styling and a more spacious interior, its drivetrain was new and improved over the Model T's. The planetary-gear transmission was replaced by a three-speed transmission with a floor-mounted shifter. The Model A's frame, although based on a pair of parallel straight rails on either side similar to that found on the Model T, was larger and stronger. Most of all, the Model A's engine, although still an in-line four-cylinder like the T's, boasted more displacement and more power.

Henry Ford and engineer Lawrence S. Sheldrick were instrumental in the new engine's design. This turned out to be good and bad news, though, because while Sheldrick offered some interesting design concepts that eventually led to improved power, it was Henry Ford's continued affection for the Model T that, in all probability, meant that the Model A engine unnecessarily shared more similarities than dissimilarities with its predecessor.

Regardless, the Model A's engine was bigger than the Model T's. Displacement was 200.5 cubic inches compared to 176.7 cubic inches. The A's bore and stroke was 3.875x4.250 inches versus the T's 3.750x4.000 inches. Even so, initial dynamometer

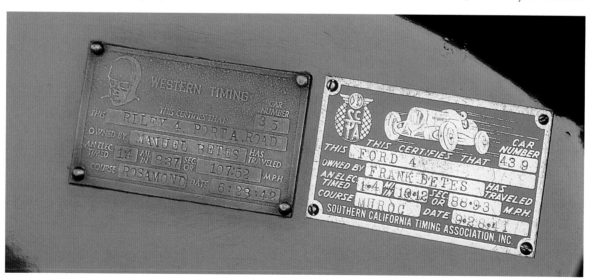

Above and Right
Other than the key fob, the interior on Manny's 1929 roadster is original. Remember, this is a 60-year-old car. In contrast, the interior to Joe Scanlin's 1929 boasts all-new vinyl, although the Auburn dash and four-spoke roadster steering wheel are indicative of what rodders did to their cars in the early days.

tests indicated that the new A motor produced no more horsepower than the T. Both peaked at 20 horsepower! Obviously, this wasn't satisfactory, and with only a few weeks before the new car bowed to the U.S. public, Henry Ford sent Sheldrick and his engineering team back to the engine room with a decree —double the horsepower.

Records show that Sheldrick had about three weeks to perform the miracle. Despite the short period of time, he came through with flying colors. The first Model A four-bangers developed 40 horsepower. The remedy centered around enlarged water passages for more efficient cooling. That taken care of, Sheldrick's team was able to improve intake breathing by fitting a Y-type intake manifold with a Zenith carburetor, and matching the engine's gas-

kets to their respective port-tunnel openings. Doubling the engine's horsepower didn't affect its reliability, either; the Model A had 1.500-inch rod bearings and 1.625-inch main bearings as opposed to the Model T's 1.250-inch bearings (rod and main).

Despite doubling its horsepower, the Model A was vastly underpowered compared to the competition. By comparison, the Chrysler's six-cylinder model produced 54 horsepower, and Buick advertised 63 horsepower for its big motor. Even Chrysler's new Plymouth, which debuted the same year as the Model A, had a four-cylinder engine that produced 45 horsepower, good for a 60 mile-per-hour top speed.

The new low-cost ($670) Plymouth also featured a hydraulic brake system. Henry Ford steadfastly refused to acknowledge the benefits of hydraulic brakes for cars, and so the Model A, like the Model T, had mechanically operated brake shoes, which required more pedal pressure by the driver in order to stop the car.

Of course, hot rodders then, as in years to come, weren't necessarily concerned with the Model A's stopping ability. Instead, their interest in Ford's new car was in how *fast* it could go, especially on the southern California dry lake beds where organizations such as the Muroc Racing Association began promoting speed events as early as March 25, 1931, when the Gilmore Oil Company sponsored an organized meet on the famous dry lake bed. And through this quest for speed the Model A race enthusiasts spawned a whole new movement among the performance parts builders.

Two of the leading parts suppliers were George Riley and Ed Winfield. As they had done with the Model T, Riley was known for his Model A overhead-valve conversions, while Winfield made a name for himself offering camshafts and carburetors for the new Ford.

Perhaps Riley's two most noteworthy contributions to the new Ford four-cylinder engines were the two-port and four-port heads. The two-port head was the earlier design, utilizing a pair of Siamese intake tunnels leading from a tubular intake manifold. The new cylinder head had two intake overhead valves per cylinder, while the stock L-block (or flathead) exhaust valves remained in operation within the engine's cylinder block. The two-port conversion was so successful at speed

Fords built before 1939 did not have hydraulic brakes. When Ford equipped its cars with "juice" brakes in 1939, the hot rodders were quick to follow. This 1929 Ford with 1932 grille has brakes from a 1940 Ford.

events that George Riley later published a booklet titled *Building the 100 m.p.h. Model A Ford* (recently reprinted by old-Ford aficionado Dan Iandola), and a brief article, "Secrets of Speed."

In his article about performance tuning the Model A, Riley wrote, "In building fast Ford speedsters and racers (and if you don't think some of the western cars are fast, ask eastern boys who have raced here), it has always been our endeavor to change standard Ford construction no more than absolutely necessary. This gives the Ford racing car the advantage of being able to obtain parts and service anywhere." In short, Riley paid tribute to the Model A's adaptability as a hot rod engine. It's simplicity and resounding

durability ensured it to be a solid candidate for building a hot rod or racer. And, by limiting the modifications to its original design, the hot rod conversion could be performed for relatively few dollars.

Riley offered an economical performance Model A cylinder head, too. It was a bolt-on flathead, offering 5.8:1 compression ratio from its 13/16-inch depth combustion chambers. The Riley flathead, which sold for $21.50 in 1930, had a combustion chamber design that was "buldged [*sic*] or curved to provide additional clearance around valves and yet the cylinder head covers a standard Ford head gasket," according to a Riley advertisement in 1931. In essence, the spark plugs were located in the center of the combustion chamber for a more uniform flame front. The result was "unquestionably the most powerful and smoothest performing flat head available for the Model A Ford motor," so said Riley's advertisement.

Unquestionably, though, it was the two-port design that a large number of Model A hot rodders sought. Three distinct Riley two-port head configurations were produced. The Model B was intended for highway use, while the Model C was for racing purposes only. Riley also offered a Model D, which was best suited for "trucks having 70 horsepower engines, with same load." (Don't confuse Riley's Model B or Model C conversions with Ford's 1932 Model B or 1933 Model C four cylinders.)

Riley advertisements of the era boasted an 80-mile-per-hour performance for an otherwise stock Model A Ford equipped with the Model B Riley two-port head. The Model C Riley head boasted more compression and more top speed (this was the cylinder head that was the topic of discussion in his 100-mile-per-hour Model A Ford booklet). All three heads shared similar combustion chamber designs; the two intake valves were positioned almost directly over the combustion chamber, while an adjoining pocket atop the L-block's exhaust valve housed the spark plug. The flame front was initiated here, according to Riley's records, to avoid pre-ignition of unburned gases as they began to exit through the exhaust port.

Perhaps the most unique feature about the Riley head is the double-forked rocker-arm mechanism that operates the two intake valves. These rocker-arm assemblies are shrouded by a pair of valve covers that resemble inverted cooking pots. The name "Riley

Steve Wickert performed much of his own engine work on this flathead. The V-8-60 has milled heads, a modified engine block, 3/4 race cam, and a single Stromberg 97 on a stock manifold.

Tom Leonardo Jr. built his 1931 roadster for about $1,000. Of course, it helped that his father's garage and backyard are stocked with literally tons of genuine old Ford parts that he could use.

Racing" is inscribed on the top of each valve cover. The two-port heads have the intake and exhaust ports on the right side of the engine. The four-port can be identified because its intake is on the left side.

There were numerous other performance-parts suppliers for Ford's new Model A four-cylinder engine. Companies such as Duray, Alexander, Cragar, Gemsa, Murphy, Rutherford and Sparks, among others, offered flathead, OHV, or single- and double-overhead camshaft conversions. And hot rodders adapted updraft and downdraft carburetors from such companies as Winfield and Zenith to specially made intake manifolds.

The Model A engine also endeared itself to hot rodders because its lubrication system could be updated to Model B (Ford) specs, giving it a pressurized system. One hot rodder of the thirties, John Athan, eventually sold his Model T hot rod to a friend, stepping up to a modified Model A to rid himself of the early Ford engine's lubrication worry. Athan, who grew up in Culver City, California, one of the hot beds for early-day hot rodding, sold his car to a young man who would eventually make a name for himself in hot rodding—Ed Iskenderian.

Athan and Isky—as Iskenderian became known by his hot rod cronies—chummed around together as young hot rodders. When Athan could finally afford to buy a used Model A, he sold his Model T hot rod to Isky (who, to this day, still owns the classic 1926-based hot rod). As Athan explains the transaction, "I didn't want a Model T anymore. I wanted something with oil pressure. So I sold it [the Model T hot rod] to Ed. Then he could worry about what it [the motor] was going to do!"

Actually, when it came to absolute top speed both Athan and Isky favored Model A engines with Cragar conversions. A Cragar four-banger was good for "about

Hot rods and race cars shared much the same speedware during the prewar years. This Depression-era champ car has a Ford four-cylinder engine with a Riley four-port conversion, a similar system that hot rodders applied to their street-going cars.

120 miles per hour," at the dry lakes, said Athan, while early Ford V-8-powered hot rods could usually muster only about a 100-mile-per-hour top speed. A major reason, of course, was that prior to World War II, few people or companies made high-performance products for the new Ford V-8, while aftermarket parts for the four-bangers remained plentiful.

Given that, the situation during the prewar years remained promising for the Model A, and later Model B and Model C four-cylinder engines, because there were so *many* performance players involved. In fact, as many as a dozen manufacturers can be listed for flathead, overhead-valve (OHV), overhead-cam (OHC), or dual-overhead-cam (DOHC) conversions alone. This doesn't include ignition, carburetion, exhaust and intake manifolds, and camshaft suppliers.

Eventually, as we'll discuss in the next chapter, the popularity—and top speed—of the flathead V-8 overtook the venerable four-bangers. Even so, today hot rod enthusiasts have rediscovered the fun and excitement to be had in building a truly fast and reliable early Ford four-cylinder engine. Today, as was the case more than half a century ago, the legendary Ford Model A engine enjoys a widespread popularity among hot rod engine builders.

But while the Model A four-cylinder engine had slipped into temporary dormancy among postwar hot rodders, the 1928–31 body has always been a favorite for transforming an early Ford into a go-fast street machine. Simply, the Model A is considered one of the all-time beautiful Ford bodies and especially lends itself to customizing. In particular, rodders tend to prefer 1928 and 1929 Model A bodies, due to the elegant look afforded it by the curved character revealed down the sides of the cowl. The 1930 and 1931 bodies look similar, but are slightly more spacious than the 1928 and 1929, and lack the cowl accent lines.

When the 1932 V-8 was introduced, many racers realized the new engine's potential for speed. They also understood that the more compact Model A body punched a smaller hole in the wind than that of a '32 Ford during a top-speed pass down the dry lake. Consequently, an early fix for making a fast roadster during the dawning of the V-8 era was to mount a Model A body onto a 1932 Ford frame that already carried a 100-horsepower flathead V-8 engine. These hybrids (as well as Model A hot rods with flathead V-8s shoehorned inside the stock frame rails) were known as A-V8s among hot rodders.

Today Model A roadsters, coupes, and Tudor sedans are considered prize catches for hot rodding. There remains a wealth of genuine all-steel bodies, but several companies offer brandnew replica bodies as well. Brookville Roadsters makes an all-steel reproduction roadster body, while Downs, Gibbon, and Wescott's are known for their fiberglass reprobodies in roadster and coupe configurations.

Best of all, though, a large number of original Model A hot rods that were built shortly before or after World War II—the hey-day of hot rodding according to many traditionalists—have survived the years, and can be seen on the road or at rod runs to this day. Many of these Model A hot rods have become recognized for what they are, rolling museum pieces that tell us exactly what hot rodding was like in the days before overhead-valve V-8 engines became the norm from Detroit. It was a halcyon time when hot rodders built four-cylinder engines that could punch 120-mile-an-hour holes in the wind, or punch a hole through the crankcase trying. Legends were made during those days, and other young men drifted into obscurity while chasing their dreams. Regardless, anybody who has ever owned a Model A hot rod will agree that this Ford is one of the most beloved styles offered by Henry Ford's company.

Antique Nationals

A favorite drag race meet among traditional-style hot rod enthusiasts is the Antique Nationals, but people attending the Antique Nats—held every year during the first weekend of June at Los Angeles County Raceway near Palmdale, California —shouldn't expect ground-rumbling diggers to numb their senses with smoking-tire runs down the quarter-mile. Remember, we're talking about antique cars here. According to the event flyer the meet is open to "only 1954 and earlier type vehicles, any engine, stock to race cars."

The event attracts a wide variety of antique cars, too. Beyond the restored oldies that show up, a bulk of the participants include early-style hot rods and former race cars, even oval-track dirt racers. Due to the wide range of pre-1955 entries, the Antique Nats have become a favorite event for people who love traditional-style hot rods.

To maintain parity among the drag racers, the event format is based on typical bracket racing, so everybody stands a chance of winning. At a typical meet there are about a dozen racing classes, plus Powder Puff and vintage motorcycles. Usually winners and runners-up receive trophies, plus a few donated prizes from supporting sponsors. There's also a custom car show that the promoters, the Four Ever Four Car Club, stage in the parking lot for hot rods and customs of any vintage.

But trophies—even winning—isn't the main draw that attracts the hundreds of participants to the Antique Nats. As Four Ever Four member Jim Siegmund once explained, "This is a real low-pressure, no-money (prize money) event."

A Model T runabout takes an excursion down the drag strip — and back through time for its driver and passenger.

Spectators are welcomed to stroll the pits and prestage lanes, where they can see the cars and talk to the owners. It's a relaxed atmosphere—just like the good ol' days!

Rightfully so, because most of the competitors are more concerned about the fun factor than their cars' quarter-mile top speeds and elapsed times. It's not uncommon to see a bone-stock Model T sedan power through the standing quarter-mile in under 40 seconds, or watch as two four-cylinder Model A hot rods face off for a sub-20-second blast!

In any case, the Antique Nats offers traditional-style hot rod enthusiasts a chance to mingle with some die-hard hot rodders, and to examine their unique cars up close. Admission to the bleachers also gets you into the pits, where the early iron and old tin sits between elimination rounds. Spectators can cruise through the pits, talk with the racers, and even take time to snoop inside the engine compartments for a close look-see at some very rare speed equipment.

The Antique Nationals isn't for everybody, nor was it meant to be. The first events were promoted back in the mid-1960s at the now-defunct Orange County International Raceway. Instead, the Antique Nationals is an event where old cars can act young again.

A couple of Model A Fords line up for the start. The racing is sort-of-fast, and sort-of-furious, and most certainly very fun.

CHAPTER 3

Dawn of the Flathead V-8: 1932

THE RODDER'S HOLY GRAIL

Practically every hot rod aficionado on this planet is in agreement about one thing: 1932 was a landmark year for hot rodding. That's because the 1932 Ford—above all other Fords and non-Fords — is the car that has carried the hot rod banner higher than any other car. Furthermore, the 1932 Ford marked the beginning of a new chapter in Ford Motor Company history—the first Ford V-8 engine.

Few people will dispute that the 1932 Ford represents one of the most remarkable body styles ever achieved by an automobile company. As a result, the '32 Ford's legend has been etched in the pages of countless hot rod enthusiast periodicals and books. One editor for a prominent, national, hot rod magazine proclaimed: "It doesn't get any better than a Deuce highboy roadster. You have that, and

Lewis Wolff built this Deuce roadster in 1963, and it won its class at the Cobo Hall Show in Detroit that same year. It later appeared in the March 1964 issue of Hot Rod *magazine. Even more remarkable, its candy apple red paint job remains intact today.*

The interior of Wolff's 1932 roadster was stitched for show. The 1962 Ford steering wheel is mounted to a traditional-style column that's been chromed — for show. The white carpet and red-and-white Naugahyde upholstery look as fresh today as in 1963 when Lewis completed the car.

you're at the top of the hot rod food chain."

To appreciate his statement, you should fully understand what a Deuce highboy roadster is, and why it's so special among rodders. First, the word "Deuce." Simply, that was the name hot rodders adopted for their beloved 1932 Ford; the Deuce was in reference to the "2" of 1932. And whenever a hot rodder says "Deuce," there's no question that he's talking about a 1932 Ford. It was the only year Ford offered this particular model—sometimes referred to as the Model B.

The word "roadster" refers to a two-passenger open-top model without roll-up windows. Due to its rather compact size, and the lack of a steel top, roll-up side windows and the accompanying crank mechanisms inside the door panels, the roadster was the lightest—and least expensive—model offered. The Deuce roadster became a prime target for serious hot rodders who preferred to spend as little money as possible (they couldn't afford much anyway!) for a car that weighed as little as possible (remember, less weight translates to improved performance).

Which brings us to the key word "highboy" in our Deuce discussion. In order to shave more weight from the car for street drag racing (popular,

Joe Scanlin restored this three-window from a hot rod that originally was built in 1956 by Ray Jones. The coupe has had several different engines, including an Oldsmobile V-8 and a fuel-injected Chevy 283. Most recently its powertrain is based on traditional hardware: a 276-cubic-inch Merc flathead delivers power to a Halibrand V-8 quick-change, via a 1939 Ford transmission with 26-tooth Zephyr gears.

but highly illegal then, as now) and to improve aerodynamics for top-speed dry lakes racing, the early-day hot rodders often removed their Deuce roadster's fenders and bumpers. Due to the 1932 Ford frame's unique configuration, the fenderless hot rod assumed a high stance on its frame rails. Thus the term "highboy".

The Deuce's signature could be found in its stylishly contoured frame rails. Up to 1932 all Ford frames had been formed around a pair of simple, straight rails. The 1932 frame was different. Ford stylists, led by Gene Farkas and Edsel Ford, pur-posely designed the 1932 frame rails to sit directly beneath the body's lower side panels. This was a major shift from the earlier frame design for the Model T and Model A. By contrast, the Deuce's frame rails followed the bottom curve of the restyled body, eliminating the need for splash aprons, as used on the Model A. To smooth the transition between the frame rail and the running board assembly, the stylists incorporated a flared character reveal, or lip, into the bottoms of the rails. Coincidentally, when the fenders were removed for racing or rodding, it became visually obvious that the Deuce's body actu-

The Ford flathead V-8, also known as the "flattie" among rodders, was produced from 1932 through 1953. A variation of the engine included the V8-60, a 136-cubic-inch motor that was supposed to replace the Model C four-cylinder. The V8-60 got its name from the design—a V-8—and the horsepower—60. The V8-60 was only warmly received in 1937, and within four years it was shelved. It was, however, a popular motor for midget race cars of the 1940s and 1950s.

Scott DaPron started with a fully restored 1932 Ford roadster to build this replica of a car that his father and grandfather raced in the 1934 Gilmore Cup. All the parts, including the cast magnesium wheels, hood straps, and cut windshield are original old parts that Scott located at automotive swap meets.

ally perched itself atop the frame rails. Rodders quickly referred to their fenderless Deuce hot rods as highboys, and the name also applied to hot rods using Model A and Model T bodies set atop Deuce frame rails (a common practice even today).

Ford also refined the rear suspension for 1932. Previous Fords positioned the rear leaf spring above the rear axle housing. To clear the Model A third member, the buggy-style leaf spring had a pronounced arch in the center section. This set the car high in the air. To lower the body for '32, the rear spring was relocated behind the rear axle. By doing

so, the leaf spring didn't require the high center arch, so the spring was flatter. By using a flatter leaf spring the engineers were able to incorporate a kick-up to the rear section of the frame, so that the body sat as low as possible to the ground. Gene Farkas, Ford's designer who played a key role in the '32's styling, used this configuration to help attain the new car's low stance. Farkas also opted for 18-inch rather than 19-inch wheels to maintain proper proportions. New-style, welded-spoke Kelsey-Hayes wheels were used. Coincidentally, these 18x3.5-inch wheels had 32 spokes.

The Model B four-banger in DaPron's roadster has authentic high-performance parts. The intake manifold is made of tubular steel and is stacked with a pair of Winfield SR downdraft carbs. Scott races the car at various nostalgia drag races. "After all," he enthusiastically said, "that's what cars are for."

Henry Ford specifically ordered the use of the old buggy-style leaf springs, once stating: "We use transverse springs for the same reason that we use round wheels, because we have found nothing better for the purpose." Henry Ford's decision, as usual, was based on the profiteer's axiom, "If it ain't broke, then don't fix it."

As the years rolled by, however, some 1932 Fords were relegated to junkyard status. Others found temporary residence in used car lots. And through time the aging Deuce became affordable for hot rodding purposes. A common practice among hot rodders of the late 1940s was to replace

the rather large Deuce body with that of a Model T or Model A. Model A roadsters equipped with a flathead V-8 became known as A-V8s. By mounting a Model T or Model A roadster or coupe (and, to a lesser degree, two-door sedan) body to a '32 Ford frame, they could further reduce weight and improve aerodynamics because the older bodies were narrower. Best of all, by slipping a lighter Ford body onto the 1932 frame rails, the hot rodders could better utilize the horsepower advantage from Ford's new V-8. The body swap required several modifications. The wider cross-members of the '32 were replaced with narrower ones to match the body width of the earlier Fords. Another common practice, starting in the mid-1940s, was to adapt hydraulic brakes (first introduced by Ford in 1939) to the highboys. The hydraulic brakes improved stopping ability, especially for the V-8-powered hot rods. In hot rodder language hydraulic brakes were commonly referred to as "juice" brakes.

To be sure, the big news in 1932 throughout the automotive world was the debut of Ford's V-8 motor. The project began in secrecy in 1930, in an engine-development facility known as the Blue Room. The engineers worked feverishly on the project and within two years the Ford Motor Company accomplished what no other car company had ever achieved—they designed, developed, and put into production an affordable V-8 automobile engine.

The new Ford V-8 engine block was based on a one-piece, or monobloc, design that required only a single casting step. Previously, most other mass-produced V-8 engines—such as Cadillac, LaSalle, and Lincoln, a company that Ford acquired a few years before—were based on two- or three-piece engine blocks. Ford advertisements boasted that the new monobloc V-8 was: "An engine with worlds of power to spare that by the very brilliance of its performance, new principles of design and construction will prove to you what advanced motor design can mean." The advertisement further claimed a top speed of "75 mph in high" gear.

Logic dictates that hot rodders quickly warmed to the prospects of utilizing the 65-horsepower engine for their forays across the dry lake beds or

A pair of vintage, military aircraft seats, a four-spoke roadster wheel, a 60-year-old tachometer, and single-piece door panels— old-style hot rodding doesn't get much better than this! Note the classic Gilmore plaque on the dashboard.

through their local back-road "drag strips." That wasn't the case. Due to its relative newness, there were few V-8 aftermarket speed parts available during the pre-World War II years. Modified Ford four-cylinder engines were capable of producing more horsepower than a stock V-8, so the hot rodders remained faithful to their little fours.

When the Ford V-8 bowed in 1932, the speed merchants had developed an array of worthy and reliable performance components for the Model A four-cylinder engine. And, since the new Model B four-cylinder (standard fare for 1932) was based on the Model A design, most of the existing speed equipment readily adapted to the new Deuce four-banger as well.

The Model B four-cylinder engine was considered a better engine than its Model A predecessor. Based on horsepower output alone, the Model B was 20 percent better, producing 50 horsepower compared to the Model A's 40 horsepower. Several factors played roles in this gain, including higher lift cam lobes, increased compression ratio—4.6:1 vs. 4.2:1—and a 1.25-inch-venturi carburetor that was force-fed by a fuel pump. In addition, the Model B's lubrication system was pressurized (first time for a four-cylinder Ford), utilizing an oil pump to maintain constant oil pressure. In short, this was a hot rod engine, but one that evolved more by chance than by choice.

Oddly, it wasn't the B-motor's additional horsepower that sparked the hot rodders' interest. Instead, it was the motor's more rugged design. The new B-four had larger bearings for the crankshaft and rods (2.000-inch and 1.875-inch, respectively, vs. the Model A's bearings that measured 1.500-inches

The interior to Hartman's 1932 coupe is finished as nicely as the body. Tan leather covers the stock bench seat and the 1936 Ford banjo-style steering wheel rim. The dash is original, with classic instruments and a column-mount tachometer.

at all journals), and the crankshaft itself was counterbalanced, weighing 10 pounds more than the Model A (despite the heavier crankshaft, the Model B engine tipped the scales at 447 pounds, compared to the Model A's 473). As a precaution to make sure that the lower-end bearings received plenty of oil at sustained high engine speeds, many hot rodders drilled the cranks to improve oil pressure to the rod bearings, and they shaved off the rod dipper-buckets, because those sump scoops were no longer needed to enssure adequate oil delivery.

While the Model B four-cylinder engine showed great promise for hot rodding, it was Ford's new V-8 that captured the spotlight throughout the automotive world in general, for no other auto manufacturer had ventured into the realm that Henry Ford

was willing to enter that year. Actually, Ford enthusiasts can thank Chevrolet for Henry Ford's decision to build the new V-8; when General Motors launched its 1929 Chevrolet model with an in-line six-cylinder engine, Dearborn's number one citizen defiantly proclaimed, "We are going to go from a four to an eight, because Chevrolet is going to a six."

Prior to that, Henry Ford had steadfastly refused to build anything other than four-cylinder engines, backing that corporate policy with his famous quote: "I've got no use for a motor that has more spark plugs than a cow has teats." Abiding by his practice to lead rather than follow, however, Henry Ford instructed his engineers—as far back as 1922—to experiment with an engine concept known as X8.

The X8 engine was an interesting design that had two rows of cylinders on top and bottom, which accounted for the X8 nomenclature. The engine was compact, and even fit inside the Model T's rather restrictive engine bay. Unfortunately, the design was fraught with flaws, among them oil-fouled spark plugs in the lower, inverted combustion chambers. Excessive oil dripped into the lower cylinders, fouling the plugs. In the end, the X8 became just another ex-program in FoMoCo's storied past. Its failure to reach the production stage further solidified Henry Ford's disdain for anything other than four-cylinder engine designs. That attitude changed quickly in 1929 when Chevrolet, with its new six-cylinder, upstaged Ford in the quest to lead rather than follow.

As with the Model A four-cylinder update, Laurence Sheldrick was put in charge of the V-8 project. Sheldrick enlisted Ford engineer Arnold Soth to pen the original design. Initial test engines were based on a rather compact design with a 60-degree valley between the cylinders. This was an ill-fated motor, giving way to the 90-degree format that ultimately debuted in 1932.

Early prototypes were designated Model 24 by Ford's research and development team, and the early prototype boasted displacement of 232.5 cubic inches. By February 1931 the new engine was ready for road testing. Ultimately Blue Room engineers reduced the displacement to 221 cubic inches, based on bore and stroke dimensions of 3.062 inches and 3.750 inches, respectively.

By 1946 the Ford Motor Company had refined its V-8. This version, the fabled 59A model, powers Wayne Hartman's classic coupe. Genuine hot rod wares include Navarro heads, a tall Tattersfield dual-carb manifold with a pair of Stromberg 97s on top.

L.A. Roadsters member Bob Dyar commissioned long-time hot rodder Dick Smith to build him this 1932 highboy in 1972. Smith did all the work himself, except stitch the tan upholstery and spray on the candy magenta paint. The car was ahead of its time, boasting several hand-machined, billet aluminum pieces such as the shock shrouds and a dash-mounted fuel-pressure-pump knob. The Halibrand wheels are real magnesium (polished), and Smith fashioned the grille insert using stainless steel sections. Truly a beautiful car in 1972 and today.

Because Ford already had extensive research data and real-world experience on flathead (L-head) four-cylinder engines, the V-8 used that configuration. In an effort to conserve money on research and development, Henry Ford instructed his design team to utilize various components from the four-cylinder engine. For instance, he told the V-8 engineers to equip the new motor with existing water pumps from the Model B four-cylinder, a move that proved to be disastrous. In this case, two pumps—one for each cylinder head—were mounted at the return-side of the engine's cooling system, which meant they had to extract hot water from the engine, rather than pull cool water from the radiator. This layout proved ineffective in circulating the coolant fast enough, and the heated water had a habit of turning to steam inside the water jackets before entering the radiator for cool down. The result was a plethora of overheating engines in the early years of the flathead V-8's 22-year existence.

Despite the overheating problems, people everywhere embraced Ford's new V-8 because it had something that few affordable cars offered—power. During the early years, if someone said, "I bought a new V-8," it was understood that they were talking specifically about a Ford V-8. For its time the flathead V-8 was considered a powerful engine, developing 65 horsepower at 3,400 rpm and 30 foot-pounds of torque at 1,250 rpm.

The original V-8 had a 5.5:1 compression ratio, and the rods and pistons turned a 65-pound, forged-steel crankshaft that rode on three main

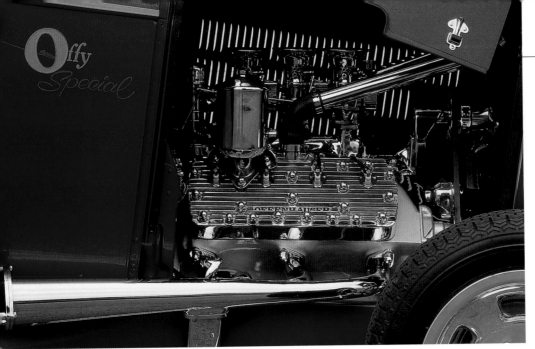

Offy Special

Literally hundreds of speed records have been established with Ford flathead V-8s, the Beach Boys rock-and-roll group immortalized the engine in their "Little Deuce Coupe" song, and countless books have been written regarding the flattie's worth as the supreme nostalgic hot rod motor.

Among the first speed merchants to offer high-performance equipment for the flattie was Vic Edelbrock Sr. Shortly after migrating from Kansas to California in 1931, Edelbrock opened an auto repair shop on Wilshire Boulevard in Beverly Hills, California. In 1934 he moved his business to the corner of Venice and Hoover in nearby Los Angeles, and about that time he bought his first car to build into a hot rod for the dry lakes. The car was a V-8-powered 1932 Ford roadster.

From the get-go Edelbrock made his Deuce roadster race-worthy for dry lakes racing. His search for more horsepower led him to Tommy Thickston, a man who designed and built Ford four-cylinder speed equipment. Thickston, with Edelbrock's help, developed an aluminum, dual-carb, intake manifold for the flathead V-8. The manifold was marketed under Thickston's name, but Edelbrock wasn't satisfied with its performance on the race track. So he set off to design and build his own manifold. The result was the Slingshot, a twin-pot manifold that used a pair of Stromberg 97 carburetors for intake. Only about 100 of the Slingshot manifolds were built before production was suspended when America entered World War II. Today original Slingshot manifolds built before the war are extremely rare and valuable among Ford flathead collectors.

Bob Dyar's Offy Special is truly special. The 59A flattie motor has Offenhauser heads and manifold. Additional high-performance add-ons for the 284-cubic-inch V-8 include an Isky camshaft and Harmon-Collins magneto. Dick Smith formed the tube headers himself, and made the stylish hood clips, along with a host of other parts too numerous to list.

bearings. The camshaft and connecting rods were made of forged steel and the self-adjusting valves—with 1.537-inch faces—were constructed of high-chrome silicon alloy steel. Early V-8s were fed by single-throat, 1.25-inch-venturi Detroit Lubricator carbs. The original design had 21-stud heads. Later editions, beginning in late 1938, had 24-stud heads, and generally are considered to be superior motors for hot rodding purposes.

But it was the company's very first 21-stud head engine that Henry Ford personally stamped the engine ID numbers "18-1" into that turned out to be a landmark for Ford and the auto industry. For that was the first of more than 12 million flathead V-8 motors to be made by America's premier auto maker. Today engine number 18-1 is exhibited at the Ford Museum in Dearborn, Michigan.

The Ford flathead V-8 is revered as the consummate traditional-style hot rod engine today.

But when Edelbrock—the businessman—built his first Slingshot manifold, Edelbrock — the racer —wasn't concerned about how much his cast-aluminum fixtures would be worth. Instead, young Edelbrock valued how well they propelled his roadster across the dry lake bed. And in 1941, only three weeks before the United States officially entered World War II, Edelbrock's Slingshot-equipped, Deuce highboy roadster was clocked at 121.42 miles per hour over Rosamond Dry Lake.

Edelbrock spent the duration of the war as a fabricator, making parts for the military. After the war he purchased his first building, in Hollywood, where he resumed business in the speed-equipment industry. Almost immediately Edelbrock returned to racing, this time with midget dirt-track cars. He designed and built much of his own speed equipment for Ford V-8s, including parts for the compact V8-60 that was popular among midget dirt-track racers during that era (The V8-60 was a compact version of the standard V-8, which, by 1937, produced 85 horsepower. The V8-60 was based on a similar, but smaller, engine block. Cylinder displacement was 136 cubic inches, and the "economy motor" produced 60 horsepower — thus the name V8-60. The V8-60 was introduced in 1937 and was offered for only four years. It was conceived as an economical replacement for the Model C four-cylinder that was offered only in 1933. Americans never thoroughly embraced the V8-60 concept, so Ford ceased production of the "baby" V-8 after 1940, replacing it with the first Ford in-line six-cylinder in 1941.). Edelbrock's speed-equipment business flourished, and today the company he founded offers a wide range of high-performance ware — including Ford flathead parts based on those that Vic Sr. developed more than 50 years ago.

Edelbrock wasn't the only name found stamped on speed parts for Ford's flathead V-8. Many of the vendors offering speedware for the Model A and B four-cylinder engines joined the V-8 movement, too. Reputable companies such as Winfield, Riley, Gemsa, Cragar, and Rutherford built performance parts for the new Ford V-8. Among the new names to join the list were Eddie Meyer and McDowell and Ardun. Today Edelbrock and Offenhauser offer a wide range of flathead parts for hot rodders building flathead motors. Eddie Meyer replica heads and intake manifolds are offered, too, along with Kong Jackson and Barney Navarro high-compression heads based on designs they perfected in the fifties. There also are several aftermarket camshafts, including the renowned Potvin (now by Mooneyes) and Ed Iskenderian's famous grind, plus ignition-update systems and many replacement internal parts to keep hot-rodded flathead V-8s on the road for years to come.

No doubt, in the beginning it was the V-8 engine that enamored the automotive community to the 1932 Ford, but it was the Deuce's unique body style that truly captivated hot rod enthusiasts during the ensuing years. After all, this was the Ford model that, for a welcomed change, emphasized form equally with function. True, the Model A was considered a quantum leap forward in the company's attention to body styling, but that car carried over some of the Model T's out-dated traits such as a square-sided, chrome-plated grille shell, cowl-mounted gas tank, and angular fenders.

On the other hand, the 1932 Ford boasted gentler, more rounded curves, especially at the fenders and grille shell. Many automotive historians suggest that the Deuce's modern (by 1932 standards) styling was patterned after FoMoCo's Lincoln, the company's luxury line leader. The 1932 Ford, experts point out, was a scaled-down version of the Lincoln, a body design that Edsel Ford also supervised.

Regardless of what experts say about the 1932 Ford and its impact on automotive history, the Deuce has become a legend among hot rodders the world over. No other car embodies the spirit of hot rodding the way the Deuce can and does. Its finely sculpted lines, its smooth, aerodynamic grille shell, and the gracefully curved frame have made the 1932 Ford a stand-out car for hot rodding. It's been that way ever since the days when the Ford flathead V-8 ruled the roost, and it will probably remain so for years to come. Life treats you that way when you reside at the top of the food chain.

River City Reliability Run

Racing wasn't the only activity that pioneer hot rodders enjoyed with their cars. They also participated in reliability runs, which were events run on public roads and highways. The purpose of a reliability run was to challenge the hot rodders' driving and navigating skills. It also gave them a chance to see just how reliable their hot rods were under daily driving conditions.

Reliability runs were especially popular immediately after World War II. In order to conserve fuel and materials during the war, the U.S. government had suspended all forms of racing. When peace was declared in 1945, many of the race associations remained in a state of limbo until former club members could reorganize to get their activity agendas back up to speed, in a manner of speaking.

Compared to staging a race, however, organizing a reliability run was rather easy. To promote a reliability run, all a hot rod club had to do was map out a route for participants to follow

Just like the old days, the hot rodders gather at the start for the River City Reliability Run. And, just like the old days, the cars are based on traditional-styled hot rods.

An open-top, highboy Model T, fat whitewall tires, and the wind in your face. Pete and Carol Chapouris experience what some people can only dream about.

over public roads and highways, issue a set of instructions for drivers and their navigators to follow, then tabulate the scores at the conclusion of the event. Scoring was based on how close the finishers' times were in relation to an average speed that the organizers had previously established. Bonus points were given if your hot rod finished in a "reliable" manner.

One of the more popular runs was sanctioned by the Pasadena Roadster Club (PRC). First held in 1947, the PRC run originated at the famous Rose Bowl football stadium. From there, it traversed the nearby San Gabriel Mountains, meandered through the Mojave Desert on the northeast side of the mountain range before terminating at a location about 130 miles from the start. Because the PRC was a chapter of the Southern California Timing Association, initial runs were restricted to roadster hot rods only. Other clubs promoted reliability runs for closed-top cars, and for the next several years this was a popular form of competition among nonracing hot rodders.

The reliability runs eventually faded from the hot rod scene, but the term "run" remained a part of the hot rodders' vocabulary for the subsequent decades. Eventually, however, the runs turned into social affairs rather than driving exercises, because hot rodders acquired the habit of parking their cars at a run site so people could check out their hot rods. Once the hot rods were parked, the run turned more into a social event or bench-racing session.

One southern California hot rodder decided it was time for sedentary hot rodders — who had resigned themselves to parking their lawn chairs — to get back in the driver's seat, so they could enjoy their hot rods for what they were built for — driving. So Mark Morton organized the River City Reliability Run to be run in the spirit of the old Pasadena Run. The first River City Run was held December 1995 in Riverside, California.

The inaugural River City Reliability Run was by invitation only, and open only to hot rods that were based on traditional styling trends. The emphasis was on two things: driving and hot rod nostalgia. As Morton's flyer stated for his first event: "Yeah, just like the Pasadena Roadster deal in the late '40s & '50s. Traditional hot rods only! No billet! No high-tech, etc. Real rods with steelies and all that."

More than 50 entries showed up for the first River City Run. And each hot rod was, as Morton prescribed, based on the traditional styles that were so prevalent when the Pasadena Roadster Club promoted its first event nearly a half century before.

The legend of Stroker McGurk lives on in Dave Lukkari's Ardun-powered modified-T roadster.

The Wonder Years: 1933-1940

HOT RODDING GROWS AND MATURES

From an economic standpoint, what occurred in the auto industry during the height of the Great Depression doesn't make sense. On the national level car sales were down, unemployment was up, yet throughout the 1930s some auto makers in America continually expanded their range of new models.

New-car sales in America for model-year 1929— the months immediately preceding the collapse of the stock market—topped 5,294,000. By 1933—four years after the world fell into economic darkness— that figure diminished to only 1,848,000. The auto industry was not without its victims. One-third of the auto makers went bankrupt during that brief period. They were joined by

Doug Kenny rescued this Model 40 coupe in the seventies. "But," said Kenny about the 1934, "it had been around for quite a while before I bought it." The five-window sports some old-fashioned, rod-building tricks, too, including independent front suspension from a 1954 Chevrolet and an Oldsmobile rear end. The body boasts some vintage styling treatments, too, right down to the 2 1/2-inch chopped top and the front and rear tubular steel nerf bars.

Not all hot rods are coupes and roadsters. Warren Hokinson spent more than three decades collecting parts for his 1935 pickup, which he built in 1990. The clean-looking pickup has a 300-cubic-inch flathead V-8 for power. The remainder of the drivetrain is based around a 1946 Lincoln transmission mated to a Columbia overdrive rear end. "Hoke" bought the truck in 1949. He paid $115.

an equally long list of insolvent suppliers and wholesalers. Practically overnight one of the largest industries in the country was on its knees and showing signs of further collapse.

Despite the worldwide economic turmoil and the hard times the population was enduring, the auto makers focused on expanding new model availability. The 1932 Ford product line featured no less than 14 different models, ranging from the least-expensive roadster to the high-end Deluxe Ford convertible sedan. Within the next nine years Ford expanded its product line to include three distinct trim levels: Standard, Deluxe, and Super Deluxe. By 1941 a customer – providing he or she

had the money – could walk into a Ford dealership and order a convertible coupe (the more rudimentary roadster was dropped after the 1937 model), sedan, or convertible sedan in at least one of these three variations.

For the most part, auto stylists were issued orders to change body features on an annual basis. The 1932 Ford – the Deuce – was a one-year style, followed by an all-new design that lasted only two years: the 1933 and 1934 twins. Despite more than 100 model changes for 1934, the 1933 and 1934 models are mainly distinguished from each other by the 1933's more shovel-shaped grille. Finally, for 1935, Ford once and for all entered the yearly styling cycle with completely revamped body lines, even though the chassis and running gear remained basically unchanged from 1934.

The 1936 Ford had even more definitive lines. Because it successfully created a new and interesting style, the 1936 has remained a favorite among hot rodders. The 1935 and 1936 Fords shared pretty much the same chassis, however, and their body structures were similar enough that hot rodders could mount a 1936 grille and hood onto a 1935 and have what was deemed a cool-looking car.

For 1937 Ford stylists showed what they had learned about streamlining, placing the headlights in the front fenders rather than on top of them. Despite the 1937 Ford's more fanciful styling, for many years hot rodders considered it and the slightly fatter 1938 the ugly ducklings of the Ford family. It was not until the late 1980s that the 1937 became an accepted body style for hot rodding. Contrarily, the 1939 and 1940 — both years shared the same basic Deluxe styling treatment, although their stainless steel trim differs — have always been well received, by regular Ford customers and hot rodders alike. When discussing the merits of collecting various Fords, one enthusiast magazine described the ever-popular 1940 this way: "Good looks make the '40 a sales leader, and the '40's fantastic survival rate is probably for the same reason."

Some people pay hundreds of thousands of dollars for a hot rod. Martin Williams was willing to spend "between $5,000 and $6,000" to build this 1936 pickup. He helped keep costs down using a stock bore-and-stroke 1947 flattie. The 239 motor has a Thickston dual-carb manifold, Howard M14-grind cam, and Edelbrock heads. The remainder of the drivetrain is old-timey, too: a 1939 trans with 1947 gears, 1940 Ford rear end, and 15-inch Ford wheels mounted with wide-whites. Check out the white tonneau cover and light-blue pinstripes.

With availability of such a diverse group of new Ford models, hot rodding and custom car building in the 1940s and early 1950s experienced marked changes from previous years. As it happened, this was the era in which hot rodders began to accept coupes and sedans as worthy candidates for hot rodding. When the SCTA (Southern California Timing Association) was formed November 29, 1937, one of its bylaws excluded closed-top cars from competing at dry lakes meets. The belief among early-day rodders was that the racing should be open only to hot rods. Because most hot rods during that era were roadsters, chances were favorable that any closed-top car (coupe or sedan) showing up on race day was probably a "stocker." Rather than waste time determining whether or not a car was truly modified for competition, the SCTA members simply limited the racing to open-top cars.

That dictum changed shortly after racing resumed during the postwar years, and eventually hot rodders began showing greater interest in coupes and sedans. One racer who helped open the door to integration among the two factions was Don Brown of the Russetta Timing Association (RSA). The RSA allowed coupes and sedans to race at their meets, and when Don Brown steered his 1936 Ford five-window coupe through the lights at 120-plus miles per hour, the guys from the SCTA raised their eyebrows, doubting the RSA's accuracy in timing. The only solution was to invite Brown to El Mirage so he could race his 1936 coupe through the SCTA timing lights. Brown showed up for the August 28–29, 1948, meet, where he ran 121.68 miles per hour. The myth was broken—hard-top cars could be hot rods too.

Stepping into this truck's interior is like stepping back in time. Owner Martin Williams maintained the Spartan flavor of a pickup, using a set of Stewart Warner gauges, gennie floor shift, 1936 Ford banjo steering wheel and rolled and pleated Naugahyde upholstery. The pinstriping on the glovebox is a nice touch.

The thing that caught Hal Peterson's attention about this 1938 convertible was its Carson top. "It's a real Carson top," he pointed out, "chopped, formed and padded the way they used to make them in the early days of customizing." Peterson isn't certain about the car's lineage, but there's no denying that this blue cruiser depicts the early days. Check it out: full fender skirts, flipper wheel covers, frenched license plate holder, original Appleton spotlights, and lacquer paint.

Another catalyst that helped change the myth was the maturity level of the hot rodders. By 1948, many of the experienced rodders were older (and wiser), and more willing to trade a little comfort for the accepted "look" of a roadster (keep in mind a roadster lacked creature comforts such as roll-up side windows and a heater—amenities that could be found in most coupes and sedans). And so cars of all styles began showing up at the southern California dry lakes shortly after the war, and at the Salt Flats in 1949 for the inaugural Bonneville Nationals.

The coupes and sedans also found favor among the street crowd; the modifications usually were for cosmetic purposes rather than to the engine. An example of a typical hot rod during that era was a particular 1936 Ford three-window coupe owned by Bob Poe. His custom treatment back in 1938 included fender skirts, flipper wheel covers, an inverted-V center section on the rear bumper (the tail-mounted spare tire was removed), and filled-in hood skirts. Recalls Poe today, "That's how we made them back in those days."

Poe's car wasn't all show and no go. He proved it at Muroc Dry Lake before the war when he made a top-speed run of 90-plus miles per hour. At that time you were among the elite when you made the 90 Mile An Hour Club. Poe still owns the bumper plaque that was presented to him by the timing association. He was member number 10.

Despite the growing popularity of the hard-head hot rods, the street crowd didn't abandon their beloved roadsters, as evidenced by a letter-to-the-editor that appeared in the first issue of *Rods & Customs* magazine, published in the spring of 1953 (as of the second issue the magazine's name was changed to its current title: *Rod & Custom*). The letter, penned by

Hal Peterson bought this 1938 convertible from Vern Williams in 1983. A short time later he re-upholstered the interior himself, using tan Naugahyde. The '40 Ford column and shifter were chromed, as was the entire dashboard and window garnish mouldings.

Most die-hard hot rodders will agree: 1940 Fords were meant for flames. Tom Clark didn't let those die-hards down. As a sign painter and pinstriper, Tom is used to working with graphics, so his 1940 Tudor boasts the full ensemble—flames and stripes, all the work of Tom's own brush. Adding to the cool look is a low stance and classic Ford wheels dressed with 1946 Ford caps and rings.

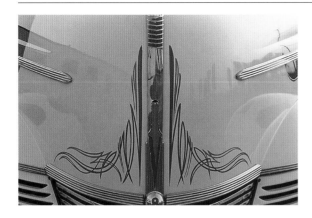

The 1940 Ford Deluxe Tudor's stainless steel trim looks perfect when it's surrounding sheetmetal is smothered in flames and stripes.

R&C reader Ron Weiskind, described a typical, daily-driver hot rod of the period:

"My home is in Seattle where I am a member of the Seattle Kustom Club. Please find enclosed a few pictures of my car, a 1935 Ford roadster. The fenders, hood, and grill [sic] are from a '36 Ford, the dash is from a '40 Ford, and the bumpers were taken from a '49 Plymouth.

"The engine is a '46 Merc and it is ported and relieved. The bore is 1/4 inch over stock and the stroke has been increased by 5/16 inch. It used big valves, a Winfield 3/4 cam, a Spaulding [sic] dual ignition and a chopped flywheel. The zephyr [sic] gears are actuated by a column shift and I have recently installed hydraulic brakes."

Indeed, the cars that Ford built from 1933 through 1940 helped usher in new and innovative ideas to hot rodding. During the immediate pre-war years, Ford introduced several landmark changes to the flathead V-8 that hot rodders would embrace. Foremost were horsepower gains, starting with the jump to 75 horsepower for 1933. Subsequent increases included 85 horsepower in 1934 and the 95-horsepower flathead intended for FoMoCo's new Mercury line of cars in 1939. The Mercury flathead interchanged with the Ford cars in every way. Hot rodders also discovered the close-ratio gear cluster from a Lincoln Zephyr readily bolted into the 1939 Ford top-loader transmission, offering transmission gear ratios better-suited for their performance needs.

Other flathead changes having demonstrative impacts on hot rodding were improved cooling for 1938 and introduction of the more rugged 24-stud head the following year. Perhaps the biggest improvement that Ford made to its cars was the use of hydraulic brake systems starting with the 1939 model. These juice brakes readily interchanged with earlier Ford wheel spindles and axles, so hot rodders could build their cars to stop as efficiently as they accelerated. It was not uncommon then—and now—to see a 1932 highboy roadster equipped with a set of juice brakes from a 1940 Ford.

These and other less celebrated advancements in the Ford product line helped change the face of hot rodding during the immediate postwar years. It is popularly noted that "change is good." And in the case of hot rodding during the late forties and early fifties, changes that emanated from Dearborn a decade earlier during the Great Depression were, to be sure, very good. Never before did so many changes (actually improvements) have such a profound effect on hot rodding as those resulting from the wonder years of 1933–1940.

Years ago blue-dot taillights were a no-no in most states. Today many state legislatures have given them the green light. Say today's law makers, "Nostalgia is cool."

L.A. Roadsters Show

As the name suggests, the L.A. Roadsters Club is an organization that, for more than 40 years, has devoted itself expressly to hot rod roadsters. And every Father's Day weekend the L.A. Roadsters promote the L.A. Roadsters Exhibition, Trade Show and Swap Meet at the Pomona Fairplex in southern California. Many nationally sanctioned rod runs easily surpass the L.A. Roadsters Show for sheer volume of entries, but there's no disputing that the annual Father's Day gathering of top-down hot rods ranks as one of rodding's finest hours.

First held in 1960 at the Hollywood Bowl, this event has become the crown jewel for hot rod enthusiasts who feel that there is really only one kind of hot rod—roadsters. And for two days every year the Pomona Fairplex is overrun with hot rod roadsters, convertibles, and cabriolets. The number of entries grows annually, and today it's not uncommon for more than 500 of the finest open-top hot rods to show up and show off.

The show itself has a colorful history, too. The initial roadster round-ups were held at the Hollywood Bowl parking lot, and by the early 1970s the event shifted to the Great Western Exhibition Center in Los Angeles. The L.A. Roadsters relocated a third and final time in 1980 to the Pomona Fairplex.

Throughout the years, though, one thing remains constant: The show continues to spotlight roadsters, where you'll find only open-top cars in the main arena. Coupes, sedans, and trucks are relegated to a separate parking lot that, by comparison, can be considered a sideshow when compared to the main attraction. There's also a manufacturer's midway where vendors hawk their new rodware. A special section remains devoted for swap meet sellers and buyers who maintain the time-honored hot rod practice of recycling old car parts.

But most of all, the L.A. Roadsters Show is a favorite and a must-go because it brims with enthusiasm—by the club members who put on the show, the guest car owners who display their hot rods, and the spectators who revel in the beauty the topless cars have to offer.

And it's this enthusiasm that has carried the L.A. Roadsters Show through the years, building it into what it is today — one of the premier events on the hot rod calendar. No doubt there will be plenty more L.A. Roadsters Shows to follow. But you won't find any of them playing at your neighborhood theater, unless, of course, you happen to live in Southern California, where this show opened back in 1960.

Held annually on Father's Day weekend, the L.A. Roadsters Show is about hot rod roadsters, and about fathers and sons enjoying those hot rod roadsters.

CHAPTER 5

Ford Hot Rods are Forever

A UNIVERSE OF RODDING OPTIONS

radition, according to one dictionary, is defined as "... customs and usages viewed as a coherent body of precedents influencing the present." As such, traditional-style Ford hot rods built today should—and do—resemble those that emerged from pioneer hot rodders' garages 50, even 60, years ago. Yet, while there can be marked resemblances between today's traditional hot rods and the "originals" that were built decades ago, the growth cycle has spawned innovations and developments that, through the years, actually improved this particular form of hot rod.

Generally speaking—from a technical and engineering standpoint—today's traditional-style hot rods have improved, but cosmetically there is little

Mark Morton's low-slung 1929 highboy has the look of a traditional hot rod. You'd never know that there's a classic Chevy 327 V-8 sitting under the hand-formed hood. The roadster boasts a wealth of styling tricks such as 1933 Ford hood-skirt louvers to accent the Model A's classy cowl curve, reshaped upper cowl section to conform to the DuVall-style windshield, a Carson-style top, and a chopped '32 Ford grille.

The tri-power carburetion—a trio of Rochester two-barrels—looks elegant when contrasted to the 1933 Ford curved hood-side louvers.

differentiation between old and new examples. Consequently, treatment to the body, interior, and wheels and tires remains much the same today as in the early years.

Many of the building techniques for a truly authentic traditional-style hot rod remain the same, too. For example, when fitting a Model A hot rod with a Ford flathead V-8 (this hybrid is known as an A-V8), purists still modify a 1932 K-member to fit the Model A frame. And a quick method to lower a Deuce hot rod is to use a Model A front cross-member, while Model A rear cross-members are typically used when fitting Halibrand V-8 quick-change rear ends to '32 Fords. Juice brakes from 1940–1948 Fords are still common transplants to

older mechanical-brake Fords. And most flathead V-8 rebuilds today still rely on a wealth of early-day speedware. It's not uncommon, however, to see a 12-volt generator spliced into the electrical charging system for improved starting and sparking.

Despite the popularity that early-Ford running gear still enjoys among traditionalists, late-model, overhead-valve engines, and modern transmissions and rear-axle members also are acceptable equipment on many of today's nostalgia-styled hot rods. Perhaps the most popular update is the use of a Chevrolet small-block V-8 for power. Ironically, shortly after Chevrolet introduced this overhead valve V-8 in 1955, it became the engine of choice among many hot rodders seeking more horsepower for their cars. Simply, the Chevrolet engine's modern design offered more performance potential than was available from the outdated flathead V-8, or even Ford's new Y-block overhead-valve motor introduced in 1954. When two of General Motors' divisions—Cadillac and Oldsmobile—offered their cutting-edge overhead-valve V-8s in 1949, the flathead V-8—a dinosaur by comparison—already was heading down that lonesome trail to extinction. Two years later Chrysler came out with its hemi-

spherical-head V-8, and within a few years Buick and Pontiac joined the V-8 club, too. These and other engines led to the flathead abdicating as hot rodding's power king. A wide assortment of speed equipment for the Chevy small-block further led to the dethronement of the aging Ford motor.

The flathead V-8 wasn't the only portion of the drivetrain destined to be replaced by new, more modern ware. By the 1960s, old Ford three-speed "top-loader" transmissions were routinely finding

This Model A roadster, owned by Joe Scanlin, was the third of three similar roadsters built by the late Dick Courtney. The styling is straightforward, even simple in execution, yet very seductive thanks to its classic composition of a 1929 body on Deuce rails. The powertrain is all late-model stuff, based on a Chevy 350 small-block, Muncie four-speed transmission, and Currie-built Ford 9-inch rear end. The windshield isn't a DuVall screen, either; this particular bug catcher was designed by early-day hot rod legend Duke Hallock.

their way onto garage floors, replaced by more sophisticated four-speed trannies from companies like Muncie and Borg-Warner. Early-Ford rear axles, too, were shelved in place of a newer, stronger third-member from Ford—the 9-inch rear end, first used in 1957. Drag racers were the first to recognize the potential of this near-bullet-proof third member. Later, hot rodders adopted it as the ultimate rear end for street use, mainly because Ford supplied the 9-inch with a wide assortment of gears that allow car builders to tailor-fit tire and transmission combinations with suitable final-drive ratios.

Eventually hot rodders began improving their cars' chassis, incorporating independent front and rear suspensions for improved ride and more precise handling. Corvette and Jaguar independent rear suspension systems were especially popular during the seventies, while the late-fifties hot rods sprouted

Bill Nielsen's modified-T roadster has a refined Model A four-cylinder for power. The four-banger has a Winfield cam and Mallory dual-point system. The Winfield "crow's foot" cylinder head is a reproduction offered by Antique Auto, and the two Winfield BU carbs were converted to be sidedrafts. The old-time headers were modified to conform to the frame, which happens to be made of 2-inch-by-3-inch steel tubing.

A side view of Mike Armstrong's Model A shows classic lines, even though the engine and body are new reproductions.

independent front suspension packages that were grafted from various postwar-era cars. A popular independent front suspension adaptation among hot rodders at that time was to mount the front suspenders from a 1953–54 Chevrolet onto 1933-and-later Fords. By the seventies entire bolt-on kits became available, using spindles, A-arms, even rack-and-pinion steering systems from Mustang IIs and Pintos. These conversions also conveniently incorporated disc brakes for the hot rods that used them.

Still, there were die-hard hot rodders who opted to retain solid-axles on their cars. They, too, could upgrade their otherwise obsolete suspension systems with four-bar locators. As the name suggests, the four-bar system uses four bars—two on each side of the axle—that are adjustable to align the axle and hold it in place. This design originally was perfected on race cars, and to this day remains popular among many street-bound hot rods. Traditionalists, however, still opt for either the split wishbones or hairpin radius rods that were popular in the early days of hot rodding.

Regardless of the innovations, most traditionalist hot rod fans today are more interested in maintaining the early-style look, as opposed to mechanical-correctness, for their hot rods. Even if a new Chevrolet 350 small-block or an older GM overhead-valve V-8 is plopped in front of the fire-

The aftermarket is rife with fiberglass replica bodies. This 1932 highboy built by Gary Moline has a Downs body on a TCI chassis. Gary wanted the powerplant to stand out, so he elected to use a 425 "nailhead" Buick V-8. Add flames, and you have one cool ride.

wall, or a four-speed overdrive automatic transmission and rebuilt 9-inch rear end completes the drivetrain, the hot rod's overall physical appearance can—and usually does—mirror that of hot rodding's glory days when men wore button-top caps and hot rods wore white wall tires.

This popularity has led to a burgeoning aftermarket industry that specializes in early-Ford reproduction parts. Demand is booming, and the aftermarket is saturated with enough "re-pop" parts that an enthusiast today can build a traditional-style hot rod using all-new parts. That includes bodies and chassis, complete drivetrains, even bolt-on goodies such as wheels and tires, headlights and taillights, and chopped windshield posts.

Based on the variety of reproduction parts, and the acceptance of non-Ford powerplants, today it's possible to build an entire traditional hot rod simply by shopping from a catalog. True, the end product is not an authentic nostalgia-rod, but it does, nonetheless, reflect an era of hot rodding that was challenging and exciting to all who experienced it.

We mustn't kid ourselves, the early days of hot rodding can never be relived. But, thanks in large part to the hard work and enthusiasm of dedicated hobbyists across the country, hot rodding's early era can certainly be remembered for what it was—a time of tinkering, exploring and learning. These Ford hot rods represent a tradition that enthusiasts hope will last forever.

The "nailhead" Buick engine in Gary Moline's 1932 highboy reflects a time when hot rodders relied on ingenuity and the parts at hand to build their cars.

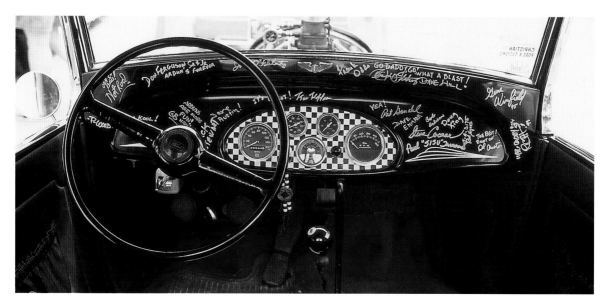

The dashboard on Dave Lukkari's funky 1928 modified Model T is dressed with signatures from many of today's hot rod legends. Their presence and conviction to hot rodding reaffirm our belief, and that is—hot rod Fords are forever!

NHRA California Hot Rod Reunion

P romote it and they will come. "They" are nostalgia drag racers and hot rodders, and every November nostalgia returns for a pass down drag racing's memory lane when the National Hot Rod Association (NHRA) holds its annual California Hot Rod Reunion at one of the oldest tracks in America, Famoso Raceway near Bakersfield, California. Famoso—better known to old-timers as Bakersfield Raceway, home of the Smoker's Car Club—hosts the Reunion so that drag racers and hot rodders from all eras gather to talk and reminisce about yesteryear. Not to be left out, there's also a full card of racing that includes nostalgia classes for front-engine top fuel dragsters, junior fuelers, altereds, and selected support classes.

But the main thrust behind the Hot Rod Reunion takes place behind the bleachers where hot rod buffs young and old can

Bakersfield Raceway used to be home of the Smoker's March Meet, where the Top Fuelers squared off every year to see who was king of the smoke. Today nostalgia fills the air at Bakersfield when the NHRA promotes its annual Hot Rod Reunion.

It's not Ford powered, but who really cares? The Glass Slipper is such a beautiful fifties-dragster that it's worth a stare.

mingle, and appreciate the sport's past rather than its future. For that reason, hundreds of old hot rods and dragsters are trailered to Bakersfield where, for two days, everyone in the pits gets an eye-full, an ear-full, even a nose-full of prime-time hot rodding. Because once you pass through the gates to the Reunion, the nostalgia intoxicates your senses, making you feel as though you just took a giant whiff of a smoking M&H Racemaster slick during a sizzling burn-out.

The nostalgia high that you'll enjoy is nothing short of sensational. On the drag strip the top fuelers are nipping at 5-second passes, with top speeds in the 220-mile-per-hour range. There are several exhibition runs down the quarter-mile steel gauntlet too. Cars like the late "Wild" Willie Borsch's Winged Express AA/Fuel Altered fries its huge slicks as it launches viciously off the starting line, or wheel-stand passes by such legends as the Hurst Hemi Under Glass or the Red Fire Engine.

Back in the pits, there's always something interesting to see because that's where the celebrity cars are parked along Nostalgia Row behind the bleachers. There you'll see all sorts of famous hot rod race cars; any one of Mickey Thompson's Challengers could show up, not to forget Tony Nancy's infamously clean orange roadsters, or Art Chrisman's famed Hustler I. The smooth

and svelte Glass Slipper, a fifties-era slingshot dragster, is a regular attraction, too. Nearby there's a vendor's row where you can buy nostalgic hot rod products and souvenirs, plus a swap meet that caters to buyers shopping for old hot rod parts and accessories. At the other end of the parking lot, the promoters cordon a special area open only to hot rods and customs belonging to enthusiast spectators attending the meet.

The Reunion also abounds with hot rod celebrities from the past. And if you don't really know who to look for, then be near the start line on Saturday when the NHRA inducts several honorees into the Hot Rod Reunion Hall of Fame. Some of the past inductees include drag racing's First Lady, Linda Vaughn; former Top Fuel and Funnycar driver, Don Prudhomme; "TV" Tommy Ivo; and one of the original Bean Bandits, Joaquin Arnett.

The California Hot Rod Reunion has been described by one NHRA official as "a romantic thing." Perhaps NHRA founder Wally Parks summed it up best when he once said about the Reunion: "That's what real reunions are all about—people remembering and appreciating good times. And that is why we're back again this year, at the Bakersfield Smoker's legendary old stomping ground where, like hundreds of other locations across the country, a lot of hot rodding history has its roots."

INDEX